DICK HAMILTON'S AIRSHIP;

OR, A YOUNG MILLIONAIRE IN THE CLOUDS

HOWARD R. GARIS

[ZHINGOORA BOOKS]

CONTENTS

CHAPTER I

THE FALLING BIPLANE

"She sure is a fine boat, Dick."

"And she can go some, too!"

"Glad you like her, fellows," replied Dick Hamilton, to the remarks of his chums, Paul Drew and Innis Beeby, as he turned the wheel of a new motor-boat and sent the craft about in a graceful sweep toward a small dock which connected with a little excursion resort on the Kentfield river.

"Like her! Who could help it?" asked Paul, looking about admiringly at the fittings of the craft. "Why, you could go on a regular cruise in her!"

"You might if you kept near your base of supplies," remarked Dick.

"Base of supplies!" laughed Innis. "Can't you forget, for a while, that you're at a military school, old man, and not give us the sort of stuff we get in class all the while?"

"Well, what I meant," explained the young millionaire owner of the motor-boat, "was that you couldn't carry enough food aboard, and have room to move about, if you went on a very long trip."

"That's right, you couldn't," agreed Paul. "And of late I seem to have acquired the eating habit in its worst form."

"I never knew the time when you didn't have it," responded Dick. "I'm going to give you a chance to indulge in it right now, and I'm going to profit by your example."

"What's doing?" asked Innis, as he straightened the collar of his military blouse, for the three were in the fatigue uniforms of the Kentfield Military Academy, where Dick and his chums attended. Lessons and practice were over for the day, and the young millionaire had invited his friends out for a little trip in his new motor-boat.

"I thought we'd just stop at Bruce's place, and get a sandwich and a cup of coffee," suggested Dick. "Then we can go on down the river and we won't have to be back until time for guard-mount. We'll be better able to stand it, if we get a bite to eat."

"Right you are, old chap!" exclaimed Paul, and then he, too, began to smooth the wrinkles out of his blouse and to ease his rather tight trousers at the knees.

"Say, what's the matter with you dudes, anyhow?" asked Dick, who, after glancing ahead to see that he was on the right course to the dock, looked back to give some attention to the motor.

"Matter! I don't see anything the matter," remarked Innis in casual tones, while he flicked some dust from his shoes with a spare pocket handkerchief.

"Why, you two are fussing as though you were a couple of girls at your first dance," declared Dick, as he adjusted the valves of the oil cups to supply a little more lubricant to the new motor, which had not yet warmed up to its work. "Innis acts as though he were sorry he hadn't come out in his dress uniform, and as for you, Paul, I'm beginning to think you are afraid you hadn't shaved. What's it all about, anyhow? Old man Bruce won't care whether you have on one tan shoe and one black one; or whether your hair is parted, or not."

Then Dick, having gotten the motor running to his satisfaction, looked toward the dock which he was rapidly nearing in his boat. The next moment he gave a whistle of surprise.

"Ah, ha! No wonder!" he cried. "The girls? So that's why you fellows were fixing up, and getting yourselves to look pretty. And you let me monkey with the motor, and get all grease and dirt while you— Say, I guess we'll call off this eating stunt," and he swung over the steering wheel.

"Oh, I say?" protested Innis.

"Don't be mean?" added Paul. "We haven't seen the girls in some time, and there's three of 'em—"

Dick laughed. On the dock, under the shade of an awning, he had caught sight of three pretty girls from town—girls he and his chums knew quite well. They were Mabel Hanford, in whom Dick was more than ordinarily interested, Grace Knox, and Irene Martin.

"I thought I'd get a rise out of you fellows," the young millionaire went on. "Trying to get me in bad, were you!"

The boat swerved away from the dock. The girls, who had arisen, evidently to come down to the float, and welcome the approaching cadets, seemed disappointed. One of them had waved her handkerchief in response to a salute from Paul.

"Here, take some of this and clean your face," suggested Paul, handing Dick some cotton waste from a seat locker.

"And here's a bit for your shoes," added Innis, performing a like service. "You'll look as good as we do."

"What about my hands?" asked Dick. "Think I want to go up and sit alongside of a girl with paws like these?" and he held out one that was black and oily.

"Haven't you any soap aboard?" asked Innis, for he, like Paul, seemed anxious that Dick should land them at the dock where the girls were.

"Oh, well, if you fellows are as anxious as all that I s'pose I'll have to humor you," agreed Dick, with a grin. "I dare say Bruce can let me wash up in his place," and he turned the craft back on the course he had previously been holding. A little later the motor-boat was made fast to the float, and the three cadets were greeting the three girls.

"Look out for my hands!" warned Dick, as Miss Hanford's light summer dress brushed near him. "I'm all oil and grease. I'll go scrub up, if you'll excuse me."

"Certainly," said Mabel Hanford, with a rippling laugh.

When Dick returned, he ordered a little lunch served out on the end of the dock, where they could sit and enjoy the cool breezes, and look at the river on which were many pleasure craft.

"Where were you boys going?" asked Grace Knox, as she toyed with her ice-cream spoon.

"Coming to see you," answered Paul promptly.

"As if we'd believe that!" mocked Irene. "Why, you were going right past here, and only turned in when you saw us!"

"Dick didn't want to come at all," said Innis.

"He didn't! Why not?" demanded Mabel.

"Bashful, I guess," murmured Paul.

"No, it was because I didn't want to inflict the company of these two bores on you ladies!" exclaimed Dick, thus "getting back."

There was much gay talk and laughter, and, as the afternoon was still young, Dick proposed taking the girls out for a little jaunt in his new craft He had only recently purchased it, and, after using it at Kentfield, he intended taking it with him to a large lake, where he and his father expected to spend the Summer.

"Oh, that was just fine!" cried Mabel, when the ride was over, and the party was back at the pier. "Thank you, so much, Dick!"

"Humph! You have US to thank—not him!" declared Paul. "He wouldn't have turned in here if we hadn't made him. And just because his hands had a little oil on!"

"Say, don't believe him!" protested the young millionaire. "I had proposed coming here before I knew you girls were on the dock."

"Well, we thank all THREE of you!" cried Irene, with a bow that included the trio of cadets.

"Salute!" exclaimed Paul, and the young soldiers drew themselves up stiffly, and, in the most approved manner taught at Kentfield, brought their hands to their heads.

"'Bout face! Forward—march!" cried Grace, imitating an officer's orders, and the boys, with laughs stood "at ease."

"See you at the Junior prom!"

"Yes, don't forget."

"And save me a couple of hesitation waltzes!"

"Can you come for a ride tomorrow?"

"Surely!"

This last was the answer of the girls to Dick's invitation, and the exclamations before that were the good-byes between the girls and boys, reference being made to a coming dance of the Junior class.

Then Dick and his chums entered the motor-boat and started back for the military academy.

"You've got to go some to get back in time to let us tog up for guard-mount," remarked Paul, looking at his watch.

"That's right," added Innis. "I don't want to get a call-down. I'm about up to my limit now.

"We'll do it all right," announced Dick. "I haven't speeded the motor yet. I've been warming it up. I'll show you what she can do!"

He opened wider the gasoline throttle of the engine, and advanced the timer. Instantly the boat shot ahead, as the motor ran at twice the number of revolutions.

"That's something like!" cried Paul admiringly.

"She sure has got speed," murmured Innis.

On they sped, talking of the girls, of their plans for the summer, and the coming examinations.

"Hark! What's that?" suddenly asked Paul, holding up his hand for silence.

They were made aware of a curious, humming, throbbing sound.

"Some speed boat," ventured Dick.

"None in sight," objected Paul, with a glance up and down the river, which at this point ran in a straight stretch for two miles or more. "You could see a boat if you could hear it as plainly as that."

"It's getting louder," announced Innis.

Indeed the sound was now more plainly to be heard.

Paul gave a quick glance upward.

"Look, fellows!" he exclaimed. "An airship!"

The sound was right over their heads now, and as all three looked up they saw, soaring over them, a large biplane, containing three figures. It was low enough for the forms to be distinguished clearly.

"Some airship!" cried Dick, admiringly.

"And making time, too," remarked Innis.

Aircraft were no novelties to the cadets. In fact part of the instruction at Kentfield included wireless, and the theoretical use of aeroplanes in war. The cadets had gone in a body to several aviation meets, and once had been taken by Major Franklin Webster, the instructor in military tactics, to an army meet where several new forms of biplanes and monoplanes had been tried out, to see which should be given official recognition.

"I never saw one like that before," remarked Paul, as they watched the evolutions of the craft above them.

"Neither did I," admitted Dick.

"I've seen one something like that," spoke Innis.

"Where?" his chums wanted to know, as Dick slowed down his boat, the better to watch the biplane, which was now circling over the river.

"Why, a cousin of mine, Whitfield Vardon by name, has the airship craze pretty bad," resumed Innis. "He has an idea he can make one that will maintain its equilibrium no matter how the wind blows or what happens. But, poor fellow, he's spent all his money on experiments and he hasn't succeeded. The last I heard, he was about down and out, poor chap. He showed me a model of his machine once, and it looked a lot like this. But this one seems to work, and his didn't—at least when I saw it."

"It's mighty interesting to watch, all right," spoke Paul, "but we'll be in for a wigging if we miss guard-mount. Better speed her along, Dick."

"Yes, I guess so. But we've got time—"

Dick never finished that sentence. Innis interrupted him with a cry of:

"Look, something's wrong on that aircraft!"

"I should say so!" yelled Paul. "They've lost control of her!"

The big biplane was in serious difficulties, for it gave a lurch, turned turtle, and then, suddenly righting, shot downward for the river.

"They're going to get a ducking, all right!" cried Innis.

"Yes, and they may be killed, or drowned," added Paul.

"I'll do what I can to save 'em!" murmured Dick, as he turned on more power, and headed his boat for the place where the aircraft was likely to plunge into the water.

Hardly had he done so when, with a great splash, and a sound as of an explosion, while a cloud of steam arose as the water sprayed on the hot motor, the aircraft shot beneath the waves raised by the rapidly-whirling propellers.

"Stand ready now!"

"Get out a preserver!"

"Toss 'em that life ring!"

"Ready with the boat hook! Slow down your engine, Dick."

The motor-boat was at the scene of the accident, and when one of the occupants of the wrecked airship came up to the surface Dick made a grab for him, catching the boat hook in the neck of his coat.

The next instant Dick gave a cry of surprise.

"Larry Dexter—the reporter!" he fairly shouted. "How in the world—"

"Let me get aboard—I'll talk when—when I get rid of—of—some of this water!" panted Larry Dexter. "Can you save the others?"

"I've got one!" shouted Paul. "Give me a hand, Innis!"

Together the two cadets lifted into the motorboat a limp and bedraggled figure. And, no sooner had he gotten a glimpse of the man's face, than Innis Beeby cried:

"By Jove! If it isn't my cousin, Whitfield Vardon!"

CHAPTER II

THE COLONEL'S OFFER

Two more surprised youths than Dick Hamilton and Innis Beeby would have been hard to find. That the young millionaire should meet Larry Dexter, a newspaper reporter with whom he had been acquainted some time, in this startling fashion was one thing to wonder at, but that Innis should help in the rescue of his cousin, of whom he had just been speaking, was rather too much to crowd into a few strenuous moments.

"Whitfield!" gasped Innis, when his cousin had been safely gotten aboard. "How in the world did you get here? And was that your craft?"

"Yes. But don't stop to talk now!" gasped the rescued aviator. "My machinist, Jack Butt, went down with us! Can you see anything of him?"

Eagerly the eyes of the cadets searched the waters that had now subsided from the commotion caused by the plunging down of the wrecked aircraft. Then Dick cried:

"I see something moving! Right over there!"

He pointed to where the water was swirling, and the next moment he threw in the clutch of his motor. The propeller churned the water to foam, and the craft shot ahead.

The next instant a body came to the surface. A man began to strike out feebly, but it was evident he was nearly drowned.

"That's Jack! That's my helper!" cried Mr. Vardon. "Can you save him?"

"Take the wheel!" shouted Dick to Paul. And then, as the motor-boat shot ahead, the rich youth leaned over the gunwale, and, holding on to a forward deck cleat with one hand, he reached over, and with the other, caught the coat collar of the swimmer, who had thrown up his arms, and was about to sink again.

"I'll give you a hand!" cried Innis, and between them the cadets lifted into the boat the now inert form of Jack Butt.

"Stop the motor!"

"First aid!"

"We've got to try artificial respiration!"

In turn Innis, Paul and Dick shot out these words. And, seeing that the other two rescued ones were in no need of attention, the cadets proceeded to put to practical use the lessons in first aid to the drowning they had learned at Kentfield.

And, while this is going on I am going to take just a few moments, in which to tell my new readers something about the previous books in this series.

The only son of Mortimer Hamilton, of Hamilton Corners, in New York state, Dick was a millionaire in his own right. His mother had left him a large estate, and in the first volume of this series, entitled, "Dick Hamilton's Fortune; Or, The Stirring Doings of a Millionaire's Son," I related what Dick had to do in order to become fully possessed of a large sum of money. He had to prove that he was really capable of handling it, and he nearly came to grief in doing this, as many a better youth might have done.

Dick's uncle, Ezra Larabee, of Dankville, was a rich man, but a miser. He was not in sympathy with Dick, nor with the plans his sister, Dick's mother, had made for her son. Consequently, Uncle Ezra did all he could to make it unpleasant for Dick while the latter was paying him a visit of importance.

But Dick triumphed over his uncle, and also over certain sharpers who tried to get the best of him.

My second volume, entitled, "Dick Hamilton's Cadet Days, Or, The Handicap of a Millionaire's Son," deals with our hero's activities at the Kentfield Military Academy. This was a well-known school, at the head of which was Colonel Masterly. Major Henry Rockford was the commandant, and the institution turned out many first-class young men, with a groundwork of military training. The school was under the supervision of officers from the regular army, the resident one being Major Webster.

Dick had rather a hard time at Kentfield—at first—for he had to get over the handicap of being a millionaire. But how he did it you may read, and, I trust, enjoy.

In "Dick Hamilton's Steam Yacht; Or, A Young Millionaire and the Kidnappers," Dick got into a "peck of trouble," to quote his chum, Innis Beeby. But the rich youth finally triumphed over the designs of Uncle Ezra, and was able to foil some plotters.

"Dick Hamilton's Football Team; Or, A Young Millionaire On the Gridiron," tells of the efforts of Dick to make a first-class eleven from the rather poor material he found at Kentfield. How he did it, though not without hard work, and how the team finally triumphed over the Blue Hill players, you will find set down at length in the book.

"Dick Hamilton's Touring Car; Or, A Young Millionaire's Race for a Fortune," took our hero on a long trip, and in one of the largest, finest and most completely equipped automobiles that a certain firm had ever turned out.

I have mentioned Larry Dexter, and I might say that in a line entitled, "The Young Reporter Series," I have give an account of the doings of this youth who rose from the position of office boy on a New York newspaper to be a "star" man, that is, one entrusted with writing only the biggest kind of stories. Dick had met Larry while in New York, and Larry had profited by the acquaintanceship by getting a "beat," or exclusive story, about the young millionaire.

On the return of Dick and his cadet chums from a trip to California, the rich youth had again taken up his studies at Kentfield.

And now we behold him, out in his motor-boat, having just succeeded in helping rescue the master and "crew" of the aircraft that had plunged into the river.

"There; he breathed."

"I think he's coming around now."

"Better get him to shore though. He'll need a doctor!"

Thus remarked Dick, Paul and Innis as they labored over the unfortunate mechanician of the biplane. They had used artificial respiration on him until he breathed naturally.

"I'll start the boat," announced Dick, for the craft had been allowed to drift while the lifesaving work was going on. "We want to make time back."

"This certainly is a surprise," remarked Larry Dexter, as he tried to wring some of the water out of his clothes.

"More to me than it is to you, I guess," suggested Dick. "I suppose you birdmen are used to accidents like this?"

"More or less," answered the cousin of Innis Beeby. "But I never expected to come to grief, and be rescued by Innis."

"Nor did I expect to see you," said the cadet.

"We were just speaking of you, or, rather I was, as we saw your craft in the air. I was wondering if you had perfected your patent."

"It doesn't look so—does it?" asked the airship inventor, with a rueful smile in the direction of the sunken aircraft. "I guess I'm at the end of my rope," he added, sadly. "But I'm glad none of us was killed."

"So am I!" exclaimed Dick. "But how in the world did you come to take up aviation, Larry?" he asked, of the young newspaper man. "Have you given up reporting?"

"No indeed," replied Larry Dexter. "But this air game is getting to be so important, especially the army and navy end of it, that my paper decided we ought to have an expert of our own to keep up with the times. So they assigned me to the job, and I'm learning how to manage an aircraft. I guess the paper figures on sending me out to scout in the clouds for news. Though if I don't make out better than this, they'll get someone else in my place."

"Something went wrong—I can't understand it," said the aircraft inventor, shaking his head. "The machine ought not to have plunged down like that. I can't understand it."

"I'd like to send the story back to my paper," went on Larry.

"Always on the lookout for news!" remarked Dick. "We'll see that you send off your yarn all right. There's a telegraph office in the Academy now. I'll fix it for you."

The run to the school dock was soon made, and the arrival of Dick's motor-boat, with the rescued ones from the airship, which had been seen flying over the parade grounds a little while before, made some commotion.

"We've missed guard-mount!" remarked Innis, as he saw the other cadets at the drill.

"Can't be helped. We had a good excuse," said Dick. "Now we've got to attend to him," and he nodded at Jack Butt, who seemed to have collapsed again.

With military promptness, the mechanic was carried to the hospital, and the school doctor was soon working over him. Meanwhile, dry garments had been supplied to Larry and Mr. Vardon. A messenger came from Colonel Masterly to learn what was going on, and, when he heard of the rescue, Dick and his chums were excused from taking part in the day's closing drill.

"He's coming around all right," the physician remarked to the young millionaire, on the way from the hospital, where he had been attending Jack Butt. "It seems that he was entangled in some part of the aircraft, and couldn't get to the surface until he was nearly drowned. But he's all right now, though he needs rest and care."

"I wonder if he can stay here?" asked Dick. "Oh, yes, I'll attend to that for you," the doctor promised. "I'll arrange with Colonel Masterly about that. And your other friends—I think they should remain, too. They probably are in rather an unpleasant plight."

"I'll look after them," said Dick. "I can put them up. One is a newspaper man, and the other a cousin of Beeby's. He's an airship inventor."

"Is that so? Colonel Masterly might be interested to know that."

"Why?" asked Dick.

"Because I understand that he is about to add a course in aviation to the studies here. It has been discussed in faculty meetings, so it is no secret."

"An aviation course at Kentfield!" cried Dick, with shining eyes.

"Yes. Are you interested?" the doctor asked.

"Well, I hadn't thought about it, but I believe I should like to have an airship," the young millionaire went on. "Down, Grit, down!" he commanded, as a beautiful bulldog came racing from the stables to fawn upon his master. I used the word "beautiful" with certain restrictions, for Grit was about the homeliest bulldog in existence.

But his very hideousness made him "beautiful" to a lover of dogs. He jumped about in delight at seeing Dick again, for he had been shut up, so he would not insist on going out in the motor-boat.

Quarters were provided for Larry Dexter, who sent off a brief account of the accident to the airship, and Mr. Vardon was looked after by Innis. Butt, of course, remained in the hospital.

Dr. Morrison was right when he said that Colonel Masterly would be interested in meeting the luckless aviator. Innis took his cousin to the head of the school, and Mr. Vardon told of his invention, briefly, and also of the mishap to his biplane.

"Perhaps this is providential," said the colonel musingly. "For some time I have been considering the starting of an aviation course here, and it may be you would like to assist me in it. I want the cadets to learn something about the fundamentals of heavier-than-air machines. Will you accept a position as instructor?"

"I will, gladly," said Mr. Vardon. "I might as well admit that I have no further funds to pursue my experiments, though I am satisfied that I am on the right track. But my machine is wrecked."

"Perhaps it can be raised," said the colonel, cheerfully. "We will talk about that later. And we may find a way to have you conduct your experiments here."

"I can not thank you enough, sir," returned the aviator. "And I am also deeply indebted to my cousin's chum—Dick Hamilton. But for him, and the other cadets in the boat, we might all have been drowned."

"I'm glad we were on hand," said Dick, with a smile.

CHAPTER III

DICK'S RESOLVE

"What do you know about that?"

"A regular course in aviation!"

"And birdmen from the United States Army to came here and show us how to do stunts!"

"Well, you fellows can go in for it if you like, but automobiling is dangerous enough sport for me."

"Ah, what's the matter with you? Flying is pretty nearly as safe now as walking! Not half as many birdmen have been killed as there have railroad travelers."

"No, because there are more railroad travelers to be killed. No cloud flights for mine!"

A group of cadets, Dick, Innis and Paul among them, were discussing the latest news at Kentfield.

It was the day following the accident to the biplane. After a brief consultation with Mr. Vardon, and a calling together of his faculty members, Colonel Masterly had made formal announcement that a course in aviation would be open at Kentfield for those who cared to take it.

"I think it will be great!" cried Dick.

"Are you going in for it?" asked Paul.

"I sure am—if dad will let me."

"Oh, I guess he will all right," spoke Innis, "He lets you do almost anything you want to—in reason. But I know a certain person who WILL object."

"Who?" asked Dick, fondling his dog.

"Your Uncle Ezra!"

"I guess that's so!" laughed Dick. "He'll say it's expensive, and all that sort of thing, and that I'll be sure to break my neck, or at least fracture an arm. But we saw one accident that came out pretty well. I think I'll take a chance."

"So will I!" cried Paul.

"I guess you can count me in," agreed Innis, slowly.

"How about it, Larry?" asked Dick, as the young reporter came across the campus. "How does it feel to sail above the clouds?"

"Well, I haven't yet gone up that far. This is only about my fifth flight, and we only did 'grass cutting' for the first few—that is going up only a little way above the ground. I had to get used to it gradually.

"But it's great! I like it, and you're only afraid the first few minutes. After that you don't mind it a bit—that is not until you get into trouble, as we did."

"And I can't understand that trouble, either," said Mr. Vardon, who had joined the group of cadets. "Something went wrong!"

"You mean something was MADE to go wrong," put in Jack Butt, who had now recovered sufficiently to be about.

"Something made to go wrong?" repeated Dick Hamilton, wonderingly.

"That's what I said. That machine was tampered with before we started on our flight. I'm sure of it, and if we could get it up from the bottom of the river I could prove it."

"Be careful," warned the aviator. "Do you know what you are saying, Jack? Who would tamper with my machine?"

"Well, there are many who might have done it," the machinist went on. "Some of the mechanics you have discharged for not doing their work properly might have done it. But the fellow I suspect is that young army officer who got huffy because you wouldn't explain all about your equalizing gyroscope, or stabilizer."

"Oh—you mean him?" gasped the aviator.

"That's the man," declared Jack. "He went off mad when you turned him down, and I heard him muttering to himself about 'getting even.' I'm sure he's the chap to blame for our accident."

"I should dislike to think that of anyone," said Mr. Vardon, slowly. "But I am sure something was wrong with my aircraft. It had worked perfectly in other trials, and then it suddenly went back on me. I should like a chance to examine it."

"We'll try and give you that chance," said Colonel Masterly, who came up at that moment. "We are to have a drill in building a pontoon bridge across the river tomorrow, and I will order it thrown across the stream at the point where your airship went down. Then we may be able to raise the craft."

"That will be fine!" exclaimed the airship man. "I may even be able to save part of my craft, to use in demonstration purposes. I may even be able, to use part of it in building another. It was a fine machine, but something went wrong."

"Something was made to go wrong!" growled Jack Butt. "If ever we raise her I'll prove it, too."

"Well, young gentlemen, I suppose you have heard the news?" questioned the colonel, as the aviator-inventor and his helper walked off to one side of the campus, talking earnestly together.

"You mean about the airship instruction we are to get here, sir?" asked Dick.

"That's it. And I am also glad to announce that I have heard from the war department, and they are going to send some army aviators here to give us the benefit of their work, and also to show some of you cadets how to fly."

There was a cheer at this, though some of the lads looked a bit dubious.

"Are you really going in for it, Dick?" asked Innis, after there had been an informal discussion among the colonel and some of the boys about the aviation instruction.

"Well, I am, unless I change my mind," replied Dick, with a smile. "Of course, after I make my first flight, if I ever do, it may be my last one."

"Huh! You're not taking a very cheerful view of it," retorted Innis, "to think that you're going to come a smash the first shot out of the locker."

"Oh, I didn't mean just that," replied Dick, quickly. "I meant that I might lose my nerve after the first flight, and not go up again."

"Guess there isn't much danger of you losing your nerve," said Paul Drew, admiringly. "I've generally noticed that you have it with you on most occasions."

"Thanks!" exclaimed Dick, with a mock salute.

Strolling over the campus, Dick and his chums talked airships and aviation matters until it was time for guard-mount.

During the next day or two it might have been noticed that Dick Hamilton was rather more quiet than usual. In fact his chums did notice, and comment on it. A number of times they had seen the young millionaire in a brown study, walking off by himself, and again he could be observed strolling about, gazing earnestly up at the clouds and sky.

"Say, I wonder what's come over Dick?" asked Paul of Innis one afternoon.

"Blessed if I know," was the answer, "unless he's fallen in love."

"Get out! He's too sensible. But he sure has something on his mind."

"I agree with you. Well, if he wants to know he'll tell us."

So they let the matter drop for the time being. But Dick's abstraction grew deeper. He wrote a number of letters, and sent some telegrams, and his friends began to wonder if matters at Dick's home were not altogether right.

But the secret, if such it could be called, was solved by the unexpected arrival of Mr. Hamilton at Kentfield. He appeared on the campus after drill one day, and Dick greeted his parent enthusiastically.

"So you got here, after all, Dad?" he cried, as he shook hands, Paul and Innis also coming over to meet the millionaire.

"Well, I felt I just had to come, Dick, after all you wrote and telegraphed me," replied Mr. Hamilton. "I thought we could do better by having a talk than by correspondence. But, I tell you, frankly, I don't approve of what you are going to do."

Dick's chums looked curiously at him.

"I may as well confess," laughed the young millionaire, "I'm thinking of buying an airship, fellows."

"Whew!" whistled Paul.

"That's going some, as the boys say," commented Innis. "Tell us all about it."

"I will," said Dick, frankly. "It's been on my mind the last few days, and—"

"So that's been your worry!" interrupted Paul. "I knew it was something, but I never guessed it was that. Fire ahead."

"Ever since your cousin came here, Innis, in his craft, and since the colonel has arranged for aviation instruction, I've been thinking of having an airship of my own," Dick resumed. "I wrote to dad about it, but he didn't seem to take to the idea very much."

"No, I can't say that I did," said Mr. Hamilton, decidedly. "I consider it dangerous."

"It's getting more safe every day, Dad. Look how dangerous automobiling was at the start, and yet that's nearly perfect now, though of course there'll always be accidents. But I won't go in for this thing, Dad, if you really don't want me to."

"Well, I won't say no, and I'll not say yes—at least not just yet," said Mr. Hamilton slowly. "I want to think it over, have a talk with some of these 'birdmen' as you call them, and then you and I'll consider it together, Dick. That's why I came on. I want to know more about it before I make up my mind."

Mr. Hamilton became the guest of the colonel, as he had done on several occasions before, and, in the following days, he made as careful a study of aviation as was possible under the circumstances. He also had several interviews with Mr. Vardon.

"Have you decided to let your son have an airship of his own?" the colonel asked, when the millionaire announced that he would start for New York the following morning.

"Well, I've been thinking pretty hard about the matter," was the answer. "I hardly know what to do. I'm afraid it's only another one of Dick's hare-brained ideas, and if he goes in for it, he'll come a cropper.

"And, maybe, on the whole, it wouldn't be a bad idea to let him go in for it, and make a fizzle of it. It would be a good lesson to him, though I would certainly regret, exceedingly, if he were even slightly injured.

"On the other hand Dick is pretty lucky. He may come out all right. I suppose he'll go in and try to win some prizes at these aviation meets they hold every once in a while."

"Yes, there are to be several," spoke the colonel. "I heard something about the government offering a big prize for a successful trans-continental flight—from the Atlantic to the Pacific, but I know nothing of the details."

"Well, I suppose Dick would be rash enough to try for that, if he hears about it," murmured Mr. Hamilton. "I guess, taking it on all sides, that I'll let him have an airship, if only to prove that he can't work it. He needs a little toning down, most young chaps do, I fancy. I know I did when I was a lad. Yes, if he makes a fizzle of it, the lesson may be worth something to him—throwing his money away on an airship. But I'll give my consent."

And when Dick was told by his parent, not very enthusiastically, that he might secure an aircraft, the young cadet's delight was great.

"That's fine!" he cried, shaking hands heartily with his father.

"Well, I hope you succeed in flying your machine, when you get it, but, as the Scotchman said, 'I have my doubts,'" said Mr. Hamilton, grimly.

"Humph!" mused Dick later. "Dad doesn't think much of me in the aviator class, I guess. But I'll go in for this thing now, if only to show him that I can do it! I've done harder stunts, and if the Hamilton luck doesn't fail, I'll do this. I'll make a long flight, and put one over on dad again. He thinks I can't do it—but I'll show him I can!" exclaimed Dick, with sparkling eyes.

Dick communicated his father's decision to Paul and Innis.

"I'm going to have an airship!" he cried. "It wasn't easy to get dad's consent, but he gave it. Now, how about you fellows coming on a cruise in the clouds with me?"

"Say, how big a machine are you going to have?" Paul wanted to know.

"Well, my ideas are rather hazy yet," admitted the young millionaire, "but if I can get it built, it's going to be one of the biggest airships yet made. We'll travel in style, if we travel at all," he said, with a laugh. "I'm thinking of having an aircraft with some sort of enclosed cabin on it."

"Say, that will be quite an elaborate affair," commented Innis.

"The question is, will you fellows take a chance with me in it?" asked Dick.

"Well, I guess so," responded Paul, slowly.

Innis nodded in rather a faint-hearted fashion.

"Now," said Dick, "I want to see—"

He was interrupted by shouts in the direction of the river.

"There she is!"

"She's floating down!"

"Let's get her!"

A number of cadets were thus crying out.

"Come on!" yelled Dick. "Something's happened! Maybe my motor-boat is adrift!"

CHAPTER IV

THE ARMY AVIATORS

Dick, Paul and Innis set off at a quick pace toward the stream which flowed at the foot of the broad expanse of green campus and parade ground. As they hurried on they were joined by other cadets in like haste.

"What is it?" asked the young millionaire.

"Don't know," was the answer. "Something happened on the river, that's all I heard."

Dick and his chums were soon in a position to see for themselves, and what they beheld was a curious sort of raft, with torn sails, or so at least it seemed, floating down with the current. Then, as the waters swirled about the odd craft, a piece, like the tail of some great fish, arose for a moment.

"What in the name of Gatling guns is it?" asked Paul, wonderingly.

"It's the airship!" cried Innis. "My cousin's wrecked airship! It must have been stuck in the mud, or held by some snag, and now it's come to the surface. We ought to get it. He'll want to save it. Maybe he can use part of the engine again, and he's out of funds to buy a new one, I know."

"Besides, he wants to see if it had been tampered with by someone so as to bring about an accident," suggested Paul.

"We'll get it!" cried Dick. "Come on! In my motor-boat!"

The speedy watercraft was in readiness for a run, and the three cadets, racing down to her, soon had the motor started and the bow of the boat pointed to the floating airship. The latter was moving slowly from the force of the current, which was not rapid here. The affair of wings, struts, planes and machinery floated, half submerged, and probably would not have sunk when the accident occurred except that the great speed at which it was travelling forced it below the surface, even as one can force under a piece of wood.

But the wood rises, and the buoyant airship would have done the same, perhaps, save for the fact that it had become caught. Now it was freed.

"Make this rope fast to it," directed Dick, as he guided his motor-boat close to the airship. "We'll tow it to the dock."

Paul and Innis undertook this part of the work, and in a few moments the Mabel, Dick's boat, was headed toward shore, towing the wrecked airship. A crowd of the cadets awaited with interest the arrival.

When the Mabel had been made fast to the dock, other ropes were attached to the aircraft that floated at her stern, and the wrecked biplane was slowly hauled up the sloping bank of the stream.

"Some smash, that!"

"Look at the planes, all bent and twisted!"

"But the motor is all there!"

"Say, she's bigger than I thought she was!"

Thus the young cadets commented on the appearance of the craft as it was hauled out. Word had been sent to Mr. Vardon and his helper to come and look at the salvaged wreck, and they were goon on the scene, together with Larry Dexter, who, as usual, was always on hand when there was a chance to get an item of news.

"I'll get another scoop out of this for my paper!" he exclaimed to Dick. "Then I guess I'd better be getting back to New York. They may want to send me on some other assignment, for it doesn't look as though I'd do any more flying through the air in that machine."

"Say, don't be in too much of a hurry to go away," remarked Dick, as he ceased from pulling on the rope attached to the wrecked airship.

"Why not?" asked Larry. "What do you mean?"

"Well, you're not on any regular news stunt just now; are you?" inquired Dick, of the young reporter. "That is, you don't have to report back to the office at any special time."

"No," replied Larry. "I'm a sort of free lance. I'm supposed to be learning how to run an airship so I can qualify, and get a license, and be able to help out the paper on such a stunt if they need me. They assigned me to this Mr. Vardon because it looked as though he had a good thing. Now that it's busted I suppose I'll be sent out with some other aviator, and I'd better be getting back to New York and find out what the paper wants me to do."

"Well, as I said, don't be in too much of a hurry," went on Dick with a smile.

"You talk and act as though there was something in the wind," remarked Larry.

"There is, and there's going to be something more in the wind soon, or, rather, in the air," said Dick. "I might as well tell you, I'm going to have an airship, and—"

"You are!" interrupted Larry. "Good for you! I'll give you a good write-up when you make your first flight."

"I wasn't thinking so much of that," proceeded the young millionaire. "But when I do get my airship I'd like to have you make some flights with me. That might serve your end as well as going with some other aviator, and you could be getting in the practice that your paper wants for you."

"Fine and dandy!" cried Larry. "I'm with you, Dick. I'll send off a wire at once, and let the managing editor know I'm going to get right on the flying job again. This will be great!"

"I don't know that there'll be such an awful lot of news in it at first," went on Dick, "for I've got to learn this art of flying, and I don't expect to do any hair-raising stunts right off the reel.

"But, Larry, there may be other news for you around this Academy soon."

"Real news?"

"Yes. You probably heard what Mr. Vardon said about his machine being tampered with."

"I sure did. And I think the same thing myself. It worked to perfection the day before, and then, all at once, she turned turtle. The gyroscope equilibrizer must have broken."

"Well, you can see what happened, for we've got her out of the water now," said Dick. "And there may be more news when the army aviators arrive."

"Are they coming here? I hadn't heard. I've been so busy getting straightened out after my plunge into the river."

"Yes, they're coming here to give us instructions, and there may be all sorts of stunts pulled off. So you'd better stick."

"I will, thanks. But I'm mostly interested in your airship. It sure will be great to take a flight with you. But there's Mr. Vardon. I want to hear what he says."

The aviator, and his helper, who had almost fully recovered from their narrow escape from death, were carefully examining the airship which was now hauled out on a level spot in the campus, just above the river bank. Eagerly the cadets crowded around the machine.

"Come here, Grit!" called Dick to his prize bulldog. "First you know someone will step on you, and you'll just naturally take a piece out of his leg. You don't belong in a crowd."

Grit came at the word of command, and Dick, slipping on the leash, gave the animal in charge of one of the orderlies to be taken to the stable. Grit whined and barked in protest at being separated from his master, but Dick wanted no accidents.

"Do you find anything wrong?" asked Innis of his cousin, as the latter went carefully over each part of the wrecked airship.

"Well, it's hard to say, on account of there being so many broken places," was the answer. "The engine is not as badly smashed as I expected, but it will take some time to examine and test the gyroscope attachment. I shall remove it and set it up separately."

"Well, it's my opinion that it was monkeyed with, and done on purpose, too!" declared Jack Butt. "And I could almost name the fellow who did it. He was—"

"Hush! No names, if you please," interrupted the aviator. "We will investigate first."

"All right, sir! Just as you say," grudgingly agreed the other. "But if ever I get my hands on him—!"

Jack Butt looked rather vindictive, and probably with good reason. For had he not been near to death; and, as he thought, through the evil work of some enemy.

The wrecked aircraft was hauled to one of the barrack sheds, which Mr. Vardon announced would be his temporary workshop for possible repairs.

The rest of that day, and all of the next, was spent by Mr. Vardon in taking his wrecked machine apart, saving that which could be used again, and looking particularly for defects in the gyroscope stabilizer, or equilibrizer. Larry and Jack Butt helped at this work, and Dick, and the other cadets, spent as much time as they could from their lessons and drills watching the operations.

For the students were much interested in aviation, and, now that it was known that the army aviators were to come to Kentfield, and that Dick Hamilton, one of the best liked of the cadets, was to have a big airship of his own, many who had said they would never make a flight, were changing their minds.

It was one afternoon, about a week following the wrecking of Mr. Vardon's machine, that, as the cadets in their natty uniforms were going through the last drill of the day, a peculiar sound was heard in the air over the parade ground.

There was a humming and popping, a throbbing moan, as it were, and despite the fact that the orders were "eyes front!" most of the cadets looked up.

And they saw, soaring downward toward the campus which made an ideal landing spot, two big aircraft.

"The army aviators!" someone cried, nor was there any rebuke from the officers. "The army aviators!"

"At ease!" came the order, for the commandant realized that the students could hardly be expected to stand at attention when there was the chance to see an airship land.

Then a few seconds later, the two craft came gently down to the ground, undulating until they could drop as lightly as a boy's kite. And, as they came to a stop with the application of the drag brake, after rolling a short distance on the bicycle wheels, the craft were surrounded by the eager cadets.

CHAPTER V

SUSPICIONS

Casting aside the straps that bound them to their machines, the army aviators leaped lightly from their seats. The big propellers, from which the power had been cut off, as the birdmen started to volplane to the ground, ceased revolving, and the hum and roar of the powerful motors was no more heard.

In their big, leather helmets, and leather jackets, and with their enormous goggles on, the birdmen looked like anything but spick-and-span soldiers of Uncle Sam. But dress in the army has undergone a radical change. The "fuss and feathers" are gradually disappearing, and utility is the word. It was so in regard to the aviators. They were not hampered by uniforms.

"Kentfield Military Academy?" inquired one of the officers, evidently in command. He looked about for someone in authority.

"Kentfield Academy, sir," replied Colonel Masterly who had come up. "I am in charge here," and he introduced himself. The army man, who wore a captain's shoulder straps, saluted and remarked:

"I am Captain Grantly, in charge. That is Captain Wakefield, in the other machine. With him is Lieutenant McBride, and my companion is Lieutenant Larson. I presume you expected us?"

"Oh, yes," said Colonel Masterly, as he shook hands with the visitors. "I'm sure we are all glad to see you."

Dick and his chums looked on with interest. The army aviators seemed efficient and pleasant men—that is all but one. The first sight he had of the face of Lieutenant Larson, after the latter had removed his protecting helmet and goggles, made Dick say to himself:

"That fellow will bear watching! I don't like the look in his eyes."

But Dick said nothing of this to Paul or Innis. He made up his mind he would learn their impressions later.

"We thought we might as well come on in the machines, as to have them taken down, shipped here, and then have to assemble them again, would take too much time," went on Captain Grantly. "Though we expect, later, to give your students a practical demonstration in how the biplanes are put together, so they may understand something of how to make repairs.

"We came on from the nearest army aviation grounds, and had a most successful flight. I must send back word to Major Dalton."

"Our telephone, or telegraph service, is at your disposal," said Colonel Masterly. "If you will come with me—"

"Excuse me, but we carry with us our own means of communication," said Captain Grantly with a smile. "We are going on the assumption, constantly, that we are in an enemy's country.

"Consequently we go prepared as though there were a state of war. We shall communicate with our base by means of wireless."

"I am afraid we can't accommodate you there," went on the head of the military school. "We are installing a wireless outfit, but it is not yet completed," the colonel said.

"Oh, we carry our own!" was the unexpected retort. "Lieutenant Larson, if you and Lieutenant McBride will get the balloon ready, Captain Wakefield and myself will work out the cipher dispatch, and send it.

"We use a code in our wireless," he went on to explain, "and it takes a few minutes to make up the message."

"But I heard you speak of a balloon," said Colonel Masterly. "I don't see how you carry one on your machine."

"Here it is," was the answer, and a deflated rubberized silk bag was produced from a locker back of the pilot's seat. "This is the latest idea in airship wireless," went on Captain Grantly, as he directed the lieutenants to get out the rest of the apparatus. "We carry with us a deflated balloon, which will contain about two hundred cubic yards of lifting gas. The gas itself, greatly compressed, is in this cylinder. There's enough for several chargings.

"We fill the balloon, and attach to it our aerial wires. The balloon takes them up about four hundred feet—the wires weigh about twenty pounds, I might say. Then we carry a light sending instrument. It has a considerable range, though we can receive messages from a much greater distance than we can send, as our force for a sending current is limited."

As he was talking the others were working, and the cadets looked on interestedly. The drill had been abandoned, and officers and students crowded up near the army aviators to see what was going on.

With a sharp hiss the compressed gas rushed from the containing cylinder into the deflated balloon. The silken sides puffed out, losing their wrinkles. The balloon gradually assumed larger proportions.

"Ready with the wires?" asked Captain Grantly.

"All ready, sir," replied Lieutenant Larson. Dick now heard him speak for the first time, and did not like his voice. There are some persons who make a bad impression on you at the first meeting. Often this may he unjustified, but Dick's first impressions were seldom wrong.

The wires, forming the wireless aerial, were carried up on two light spreaders, hanging down from a network that went over the balloon bag. From the aerials depended the wires that were attached to the receiving and sending apparatus. These wires were on a reel, and would he uncoiled as the balloon arose. The earth-end would be attached to the telephone receivers and to the apparatus, consisting of a spark-gap wheel and other instruments designed to send into space the electrical impulses that could be broken up into dots, dashes and spaces, spelling out words according to the Morse or Continental code—whichever was used.

Captain Grantly looked over everything. His assistants signified that every connection was made.

"Send her up," ordered the commander, and as the catch, holding the balloon, was released the spherical bag of gas shot into the air, carrying with it the aerials, and unreeling the connecting wires.

Quickly it rose to nearly five hundred feet, and, when it had been anchored, all was soon in readiness.

Meanwhile a code dispatch had been written out, and as it was handed to Captain Wakefield, who was to operate the wireless, he began depressing the key that made and broke the electrical current. The current itself came from a small, but powerful, storage battery, and it had been switched on. The current also set in motion a toothed wheel of brass. This wheel revolved on its axis with the points, or teeth, passing rapidly in front of a platinum contact point.

As each tooth thus came in opposition to the point, a blue spark of electricity would shoot out with a vicious snap; that is if the connection key were pressed down. If the key were not depressed no current flowed.

I presume most of you understand how the wireless works, so I will not give you a complete description save to say that it is just like a telegraph system, in fundamentals. The only difference is that no connecting metallic wires are needed between stations.

A group of wires in parallels, called "aerials," are hung in the air at one point, or station, and a similar set is suspended at the other station. The electrical current jumps through the air from one group of wires to the other, without being directly connected, hence the name "wireless," though really some wires are used.

The electrical impulse can be sent for thousands of miles through the air, without any directly connecting wires. And the method of communication is by means of dots, dashes and spaces.

You have doubtless heard the railroad or other telegraph instruments clicking. You can hold your table knife blade between two tines of your fork, and imitate the sound of the telegraph very easily.

If you move your knife blade up and down once, quickly, that will represent a dot. If you move it more slowly, holding it down for a moment, that would be a dash. A space would be the interval between a dot and a dash, or between two dots or two dashes.

Thus, by combinations of dots, dashes and spaces, the letters of the alphabet may be made and words spelled out. For instance a dot and a dash is "A."

In telegraphing, of course, the operator listens to the clicking of the brass sounder in front of him on the desk. But in wireless the electrical waves, or current received, is so weak that it would not operate the sounder. So a delicate telephone receiver is used. This is connected to the receiving wires, and as the sender at his station, perhaps a thousand miles away, presses down his key, and allows it to come up, thus making dots, dashes and spaces, corresponding clicks are made in the telephone receiver, at the ear of the other operator.

It takes skill to thus listen to the faint clicks that may be spelled out into words, but the operators are very skillful. In sending messages a very high tension current is needed, as most of it is wasted, leaping through the air as it does. So that though the clicks may sound very loud at the sending apparatus, and the blue sparks be very bright, still only faint clicks can be heard in the head-telephone receiver at the other end.

"You may send," directed Captain Grantly to Captain Wakefield, and the blue sparks shot out in a dazzling succession, as the spiked wheel spun around. This was kept up for some little time, after the receiving operator at the army headquarters had signified that he was at attention. Then came a period of silence. Captain Wakefield was receiving a message through space, but he alone could hear this through the telephone receiver.

He wrote it out in the cipher code, and soon it was translated.

"I informed them that we had arrived safely," said Captain Grantly to Colonel Masterly, "and they have informed me that we are to remain here until further notice, instructing your cadets in the use of the aircraft."

"And we are very glad to have you here," replied the commandant of Kentfield. "If you will come with me I will assign you to quarters."

"We had better put away our biplanes, and haul down our wireless outfit," suggested Captain Grantly.

"Allow me to assign some of the cadets to help you," suggested the colonel, and this offer being accepted, Dick, to his delight, was one of those detailed, as were Innis and Paul.

Giving his instructions to the two lieutenants, Captain Grantly, with the junior captain, accompanied Colonel Masterly to the main buildings of the Academy.

"Well, let's dig in, and get through with this job," suggested Lieutenant Larson, in surly tones to his companion. "Then I'm going to ask for leave and go to town. I'm tired."

"So am I, but we've got to tighten up some of those guy wires. They are loose and need attention. They might order a flight any time," his fellow lieutenant said.

"Well, you can stay and tighten 'em if you like. I'm not," was the growling retort. "I'm sick of this business anyhow! Let some of the kids do the work."

"They don't know how," was the good-natured answer of Lieutenant McBride.

"There is a professional aviator here now," said Dick, as he recalled Mr. Vardon. "We might get him to help you."

"I don't care," said Lieutenant Larson, as he began hauling down the suspended balloon. "I only know I'm sick of so much work. I think I'll go back into the artillery."

Dick and his chums naturally did not care much for the surly soldier, but they liked Lieutenant McBride at once. He smilingly told them what to do, and the boys helped to push the machines to a shed that had been set aside for them. The wireless apparatus was taken apart and stored away, the gas being let out of the balloon.

The work was almost finished, when Larry Dexter, with Mr. Vardon and the latter's helper, Jack, came across to the sheds. They had come to see the army airships.

By this time Lieutenant Larson had finished what he considered was his share of the work, and was on his way to get a brief leave of absence from his captain. At the entrance to the shed he came face to face with Mr. Vardon and Jack.

"Oh, so you're the professional aviator they spoke of," said Larson, with a sneer in his tone.

"Yes, I'm here," replied Mr. Vardon, quietly. "I did not expect to see you here, though."

"The surprise is mutual," mocked the other. "I read about your failure. I suppose now, you will quit fooling with that gyroscope of yours, and give my method a trial."

"I never will. I am convinced that I am right, and that you are wrong."

"You're foolish," was the retort.

Jack Butt stepped forward and whispered in the ear of his employer, so that at least Dick heard what he said.

"I believe HE did it!" were the tense words of the machinist.

CHAPTER VI

DICK'S FIRST FLIGHT

Mr. Vardon gave his helper a quick and warning glance.

"Hush!" he exclaimed, as he looked to see if Lieutenant Larson had heard what Jack had said. But the army man evidently had not. He gave the machinist a glance, however, that was not the most pleasant in the world. It was evident that there was some feeling between the two. Dick wondered what it was, and what Jack's ominous words meant.

Having put away the two biplanes, and requested the cadets to look at them as much as they liked, but not to meddle with the apparatus, the two lieutenants left the sheds, to report to their respective captains. Mr. Vardon and his helper remained with Dick and his chums.

"Very fine machines," said the aviator. "Compared to my poor pile of junk, very fine machines indeed!"

"But part of yours is good; isn't it?" asked Dick. "You can use part of it, I should think."

"Very little," was the hopeless reply. "The damage was worse than I thought. My gyroscope attachment is a total wreck, and it will cost money to build a new one."

"Yes, and that gyroscope was tampered with before we started on this last flight!" declared Jack, with conviction. "And I'm sure HE did it!" he added, pointing an accusing finger at the retreating form of Lieutenant Larson.

"You must not say such things!" cried the aviator. "You have no proof!"

"I have all the proof I want as far as he is concerned," declared Jack. "Maybe he didn't intend to kill us, or hurt us, but he sure did want to wreck the machine when he tampered with the gyroscope."

"What is the gyroscope?" asked Dick.

"It is an invention of mine, and one over which Lieutenant Larson and I had some argument," said Mr. Vardon.

"You probably know," the aviator went on, while Dick, Paul, and Innis, with several other cadets, listened interestedly, "you probably know that one of the great problems of aviation is how to keep a machine from turning turtle, or turning over, when it strikes an unexpected current, or 'air pocket' in the upper regions. Of course a birdman may, by warping his wings, or changing the elevation of his rudder, come out safely, but there is always a chance of danger or death.

"If there was some automatic arrangement by which the airship would right itself, and take care of the unexpected tilting, there would be practically no danger.

"I realized that as soon as I began making airships, and so I devised what I call a gyroscope equilibrizer or stabilizer. A gyroscope, you know, is a heavy wheel, spinning at enormous speed, on an anti-friction axle. Its great speed tends to keep it in stable equilibrium, and, if displaced by outside forces, it will return to its original position.

"You have probably seen toy ones; a heavy lead wheel inside a ring. When the wheel is spinning that, and the ring in which it is contained, may be placed in almost any position, on a very slender support and they will remain stable, or at rest.

"So I put a gyroscope on my airship, and I found that it kept the machine in a state of equilibrium no matter what position we were forced to take by reason of adverse currents. Of course it was not an entire success, but I was coming to that.

"In the biplane which was wrecked in the river I had my latest gyroscope. It seemed to be perfect, and, with Jack and Harry, I had made a number of beautiful flights. I even flew alone upside down, and had no trouble.

"Before that I had made the acquaintance of Lieutenant Larson, who is also an expert aviator. He worked for me before he went in the army. He had his own ideas about equilibrium, and his plan, which he wanted me to adopt, consists of tubes of mercury that can automatically be tilted at different angles. I do not believe they will ever work, and I told him so. I refused to use them, and he and I parted, not the best of friends. He wanted his invention exploited, but I refused to try it, as I thought it dangerous.

"When my gyroscope worked fairly well, I presume Lieutenant Larson was professionally jealous. At any rate he, left me, and I am glad of it."

"But he was around our workshop just before we made this last flight!" insisted Jack. "He came in pretending he had left some of his important drawings behind when he went away, but I noticed that he hung around the airship a good bit. I saw him looking at, and running the gyroscope, and I'm sure he did something to it that caused it to fail to work, and so wrecked us."

"You should not say such things," chided Mr. Vardon.

"Well, I believe it's true," insisted Jack. "And you found something wrong with the gyroscope, when you took it from the airship; didn't you?"

"Yes, but that may have occurred in the wreck."

"No, that gyroscope began to act wrong before we started to fall," went on the helper. "I noticed it, and I believe that mean lieutenant monkeyed with it. He wanted you to think your plans were failures."

"I should dislike to believe that of anyone," spoke Mr. Vardon, seriously.

"Well, I'm going to keep my eye on him," said Jack. "He won't get another chance at any of our machines."

It was a day or so after this conversation that Dick came upon his chum Innis, talking to Mr. Vardon. They seemed very much in earnest, and at Dick's approach the aviator strolled away. Innis stood regarding him a moment, and remarked, in a low tone:

"Poor chap!"

"What's the trouble?" asked Dick, quickly. "Has anything happened to him?"

"Yes, Dick, a whole lot of things!" replied Innis earnestly. "I feel mighty sorry for him. You know how his airship was wrecked, but that's only one of his troubles. He's practically lost every cent he has in the world, and he's deeply in debt, for he borrowed money to build his aircraft, and perfect his stabilizer. He's just about down and out, poor chap, and he feels mighty blue, I can tell you.

"When you came up I was just trying to figure out a way to help him. But I don't see how I can. My dad hasn't any too much money himself, since some of his investments failed, or he'd pull my cousin out of this hole. But, as it is, I don't see what's to be done. And his gyroscope stabilizer will work, too, only he won't get a chance to prove it, now."

Dick was silent a moment, and then he asked:

"Say, Innis, would it help your cousin any if he had a contract to build airships, and could install his stabilizer on one of them?"

"Why, of course it would, Dick! That would be just the very thing he'd want. But who'd give him such a contract, especially after this accident? And he hasn't any money to back up his claims. In fact he's a bankrupt. Nobody would give him such a chance."

"Yes, I think someone would," said Dick, quietly.

"Who?" asked Innis, quickly.

"I would. It's this way," the young millionaire went on. "I've fully made up my mind to have an airship, since dad consented, though I believe he's secretly laughing at me. Now the kind of craft I want doesn't come ready made—it will have to be built to order.

"So why can't I contract with your cousin to make my airship for me? I'd be willing to pay all expenses and whatever his services were worth, so he could make some money that way. I'd a good deal rather give him a chance on the work, than some stranger. Besides, I like his idea of a gyroscope, and, even if he doesn't want to build my craft, I'd like to arrange to buy one of his stabilizers. Do yon think he would like to take the contract from me?"

"Do I?" cried Innis earnestly. "Say, he'll jump at the chance! You try him, and see! Say, this is fine of you, old man!"

"Oh, nonsense! It isn't anything of the sort," protested Dick. "I've got to have somebody build my airship, and I'd rather it would be your cousin than anyone else."

"It's fine and dandy!" Innis exclaimed. "Come on; let's find him and tell him. He needs something to cheer him up, for he's got the blues horribly. Come along, Dick."

To say that Mr. Vardon was delighted to accept Dick's offer is putting it mildly. Yet he was not too demonstrative.

"This is the best news I've heard in a long while," he said. "I guess my cousin has told you I'm pretty badly embarrassed financially," he added.

"Yes," assented Dick. "Well, I happen to have plenty of money, through no fault of my own, and we'll do this airship business up properly.

"I'd like you to get started at it as soon as you can, and as there will be preliminary expenses, I'm going to advance you some cash. You'll have to order certain parts made up, won't you?" he asked.

"Yes, I presume so," agreed the aviator.

"And, of course, I'll want your stabilizer on my craft."

"That's very good of you to say. It will give me a fine chance to demonstrate it," said Mr. Vardon.

Later in the day, Dick, his chums, the aviator and Larry Dexter were talking about some of the flights made in the army machines that afternoon.

"Can you arrange to have a wireless outfit on my airship?" asked the young millionaire, as an exchange of wireless talk had been a feature of the exhibition that day.

"Oh, yes, that can easily be done," assented the birdman.

"Say, you're going to have a fine outfit!" complimented Paul.

"Might as well have a good one while I'm at it," answered Dick, with a laugh. "I've got to make good on dad's account anyhow. I can't stand him laughing at me. I wish I had my airship now."

"I'll start building it, soon," promised Mr. Vardon.

"I'll want it in time for the summer vacation," went on Dick. "I'm going to spend a lot of time in the air."

"Why don't you make a try for the prize?" suggested Mr. Vardon.

"What prize?" Dick wanted to know.

"Why the United States Government, to increase interest in airship navigation, and construction, especially for army purposes, has offered a prize of twenty thousand dollars for the first flight from the Atlantic to the Pacific, or from New York to San Francisco, by an airship carrying at least three persons. Only two landings are allowed during the flight, to take on gasolene, or make repairs. Why don't you try for that?"

"What, me try for that prize in the first airship I ever owned!" exclaimed Dick. "I wouldn't have the nerve! I guess the government doesn't want amateurs in the transcontinental flight."

"It doesn't make a bit of difference," declared Mr. Vardon. "It is going to be an open competition. And, let me tell you, amateurs have done as much, if not more, than the professionals, to advance and improve aviation. Why, as a matter of fact, we're all amateurs. We are learning something new every day. The art, or business, of flying is too new to have in it anything but amateurs. Don't let that stop you, Dick."

"Well, I'll think about it," said the young millionaire.

Dick obtained some detailed information, and entry blanks for the government prize contest, and a little later announced to his chums:

"Well, fellows, in view of what Mr. Vardon said about amateurs, maybe I will have a try for that prize. It will give us an object, instead of merely flying aimlessly about. And if I should win, wouldn't I have the laugh on dad! Yes, I'll make a try for it!" he added.

"And we'll help you!" cried Paul.

"And I'll make a good story of it," promised Larry Dexter.

"I guess we'd better get the airship first," suggested Innis, dryly.

"Oh, I'll look after that," promised his aviator cousin.

The days that followed were busy ones at Kentfield Academy. A course of instruction was arranged concerning the making and flying of airships. In the former Mr. Vardon was the chief lecturer, as he had had more practical experience in building the aircraft than had either of the army captains.

But the army men had made a study of air currents, and the management of biplanes and monoplanes, and were equal to Mr. Vardon in this respect. And so the cadets looked on and listened, watching the army aviators test their machines, run them over the starting ground, and finally, by a tilting of the rudders, send the machines up like big birds.

"Young gentlemen," announced Colonel Masterly after chapel exercises one morning, "I have an important announcement to make. You have been studying aviation for some time now, and it is necessary, if you keep on with it, to have practical work. Therefore we have decided that, taking turns, those cadets in this course will make a flight, beginning with today. You will go up, one in each aeroplane, with the two army officers, who will look after and instruct you.

"I will now call for volunteers to make the first flight. Don't all speak at once," added the colonel, with a grim smile.

There was a moment of breathless pause, and then, from where he sat, Dick arose. With a salute he said:

"I'll volunteer, sir."

"Good!" came in whispered comment that the colonel did not try to check.

"And I'll also volunteer!" spoke Innis, quickly.

"So will I!" added Paul, and then several more announced their intention.

That afternoon came around very quickly, it seemed. Out on the starting ground were the two big machines, being looked over by the army men. The cadets were drawn up in files.

"All ready, sir," announced Captain Grantly to Major Rockford. "The first cadet will take his place."

"Dick Hamilton!" called the commandant, and our hero stepped forward for his first airship flight.

CHAPTER VII

A QUEER LANDING

"Now don't get nervous," said Captain Grantly to Dick, with a grim smile, as the young millionaire took his seat in the place provided for the third occupant of the biplane.

"Well, I'll try my best," answered Dick, smiling ruefully. "Am I to do anything?"

"Not a thing," Captain Grantly assured him. "Just sit still; that's all."

Dick rather wished he could have gone in the other machine, for he had no liking for the surly lieutenant with the captain. But Dick had been assigned to this craft, and military rules prevailed at Kentfield. You did as you were told without question.

Dick took his place, and watched with interest the operations of Captain Grantly and his lieutenant. Whatever one thought of the latter, personally, it must be admitted that he knew his business when it came to airships. In some matters even his superior officer, Captain Grantley, deferred to the judgment of Larson.

"You won't have to do a thing," went on the lieutenant to Dick. "Just sit still, and, above all, no matter what happens, don't touch any of the wheels or levers."

"No, that might wreck us," added the captain.

"We'll manipulate the machine, at the same time telling you, and showing you, how to do it. In time you will run it yourself, with us looking on, and I believe it is the intention of Colonel Masterly to have you cadets finally operate a machine on your own responsibility."

"I hope I may learn to do so," spoke Dick, "for I'm going to have a craft of my own."

"Are you indeed?" asked the captain, interestedly. "It's rather an expensive pleasure—not like automobiling."

"Well, luckily or not, I happen to have plenty of money," said Dick. "I'm going to have quite a large machine built."

Was it fancy, or did Lieutenant Larson look at Dick with peculiar meaning in his rather shifty eyes. Dick, however, was too much occupied in the coming flight to pay much attention to this.

"If you're going to have a machine, perhaps you're going to have a try for the twenty thousand dollar prize," suggested Captain Grantly, as he tested the gasolene and spark levers, and looked at several turn-buckles which tightened the guy wires.

"Well, I have about decided to," answered Dick, looking over at the other aircraft, in which Paul Drew was to make an ascent.

"Jove! I wish I had that chance!" exclaimed Larson. "I'm sure, with my mercury balancer I could—"

"There you go again!" cried Captain Grantly. "I tell you your idea is all wrong about that balancer! Wing warping is the only proper way."

"But that isn't automatic, and what is needed is an automatic balancer or equilibrizer," insisted the lieutenant.

"Well, we won't discuss it now," went on the captain. "Are you all ready, Mr. Hamilton?"

"All ready, yes, sir."

The captain and Lieutenant Larson took their places, one on either side of Dick. Some of the orderlies at the Academy had been detailed to assist in the start, holding back on the biplane until the engine had attained the necessary speed.

There was an arrangement whereby the machine could be held in leash, as it were, by a rope, and when the necessary pressure developed from the propeller blades, the rope could be loosed from the aviator's seat. But that attachment was not in use at Kentfield then.

The powerful motor hummed and throbbed, for a muffler was temporarily dispensed with on account of its weight. Every unnecessary ounce counts on an airship, as it is needful to carry as much oil and gasolene as possible, and the weight given over to a muffler could be more advantageously applied to gasolene, on the smaller craft.

Faster and faster whirled the big blades, cutting through the air. The captain kept his eyes on a balance scale, by which was registered the pull of the propellers.

"That's enough!" he cried. "Let her go!"

Dick felt the machine move slowly forward on the rubber tired bicycle wheels over the grassy starting ground, gradually acquiring speed before it would mount upward into the air.

Perhaps a word of explanation about airships may not be out of place. Those of you who know the principle on which they work, or who have seen them, may skip this part if you wish.

The main difference between a balloon and an aeroplane, is that the balloon is lighter than air, being filled with a very light gas, which causes it to rise.

An aeroplane is heavier than air, and, in order to keep suspended, must be constantly in motion. The moment it stops moving forward it begins to fall downward.

There are several kinds of airships, but the principle ones are monoplanes and biplanes. Mono means one, and monoplane has but one set of "wings," being built much after the fashion of a bird.

A biplane, as the name indicates, consists of two sets of planes, one above the other. There are some triplanes, but they have not been very successful, and there are some freak aeroplanes built with as many as eight sets.

If you will scale a sheet of tin, or a thin, flat stone, or even a slate from a roof, into the air, you will have the simplest form of an aeroplane. The stone, or tin, is heavier than the amount of air it displaces, but it stays up for a comparatively long time because it is in motion. The moment the impulse you have given it by throwing fails, then it begins to fall.

The engine, or motor, aboard an aeroplane keeps it constantly in motion, and it glides along through the air, resting on the atmosphere, by means of the planes or wings.

If you will take a clam shell, and, holding it with the concave side toward the ground, scale it into the air, you will see it gradually mount upward. If you hold the convex side toward the ground and throw it, you will see the clam shell curve downward.

That is the principle on which airships mount upward and descend while in motion. In a biplane there is either a forward or rear deflecting rudder, as well as one for steering from side to side. The latter works an the same principle as does the rudder of a boat in the water. If this rudder is bent to the right, the craft goes to the right, because of the pressure of air or water on the rudder twisted in that direction. And if the rudder is deflected to the left, the head of the craft takes that direction.

Just as the curve of a clam shell helps it to mount upward, so the curve of the elevating or depressing rudder on an airship helps it to go up or down. If the rudder is inclined upward the aeroplane shoots toward the clouds. When the rudder is parallel to the plane of the earth's surface, the airship flies in a straight line. When the rudder is tilted downward, down goes the craft.

I hope I have not wearied you with this description, but it was, perhaps, needful, to enable those who have never seen an aeroplane to understand the working principle. One point more. A gasolene motor, very powerful, is used to whirl the wooden propeller blades that shove the airship through the air, as the propeller of a motor-boat shoves that craft through the water.

Faster and faster across the grassy ground went the biplane containing Dick Hamilton and the army officers. It was necessary to get this "running start" to acquire enough momentum so that the craft would rise, just as a heavy bird has sometimes to run along the ground a few steps before its wings will take it up.

"Here we go!" suddenly exclaimed the captain, and as he raised the elevating rudder the big craft slowly mounted on a slant.

Dick caught his breath sharply as he felt himself leaving the earth. He had once gone up in a captive balloon at a fair, but then the earth seemed sinking away beneath him. This time it seemed that he was leaving the earth behind.

Higher and higher they went, and Dick could feel the strong wind in his face. His eyes were protected by goggles, made of celluloid to avoid accidents from broken glass in case of a fall, and on his head he wore a heavy leather helmet, not unlike those used by football players. He was strapped to his seat, as were the others, in case the machine should turn turtle. The straps would then prevent them from falling out, and give them a chance to right the craft.

For this can be done, and now some aviators practice plying upside down to get used to doing it in case they have to by some accidental shift of the wind. Some of them can turn complete somersaults, though this is mostly done in monoplanes, and seldom in a biplane, which is much more stable in the air.

"Feel all right?" asked Captain Grantly of Dick. He asked this, but Dick could not hear a word, on account of the great noise of the motor. But he could read the officer's lip motions.

"Yes, I'm all right," the young millionaire nodded back.

He was surprised to find, that, after that first sinking sensation at the pit of his stomach, he was not afraid. He now felt a glorious sense of elation and delight.

He was actually flying, or the next thing to it.

"We'll go a little higher," said the captain, as he elevated the rudder a little more. The aeroplane kept on ascending. Dick looked down. He did not feel dizzy as he had half expected. Far below him were the buildings of Kentfield, and the green parade ground. But what were those things like little ants, crawling over the campus?

Why the cadets, of course! They looked like flies, or specks. Dick was ready to laugh.

On a level keel they now darted ahead at greater speed as Lieutenant Larson turned on more gasolene. Then, when Dick had become a little used to the novel sensation, they showed him how to work the different levers. The motor was controlled by spark and gasolene exactly as is an automobile. But there was no water radiator, the engine being an up-to-date rotating one, and cooling in the air. The use of the wing-warping devices, by which the alerons, or wing-tips are "warped" to allow for "banking" in going around a curve, were also explained to Dick by means of the levers controlling them.

You know that a horse, a bicyclist, or a runner leans in toward the centre of the circle in making a curve. This is called "banking" and is done to prevent the centrifugal force of motion from taking one off in a straight line. The same thing must be done in an airship. That is, it must be inclined at an angle in making a curve.

And this is accomplished by means of bending down the tips of the planes, pulling them to the desired position by means of long wires. It can also he accomplished by small auxiliary planes, called alerons, placed between the two larger, or main, planes. There is an aleron at the end of each main wing.

Straight ahead flew the army men and Dick, and then, when the cadet was more used to it, they went around on a sharp curve. It made the young millionaire catch his breath, at first, for the airship seemed to tilt at a dangerous angle. But it was soon righted and straightened out again.

Suddenly a shadow seemed to pass over Dick's head. He looked up, thinking it was a dark cloud, low down, but, to his surprise, it was the other army craft flying above them.

"A race!" thought Dick, and he wondered how his chum Paul was faring.

There was an impromptu race between the two aircraft, and then they separated, neither one gaining much advantage. Back and forth they went, over the school grounds, and then in circles. Dick was rapidly acquiring knowledge of how to operate the big biplane.

"We'll go down now!" spoke the captain, though Dick could not hear the words. The young millionaire made up his mind that he would have a muffler on his airship, and also more room to move about. He intended to make rather a long flight.

The deflecting rudder was tilted downward, and the descent began. They were some distance out from the Kentfield grounds now, but were headed for them on a long slant. Dick wondered if they would reach them.

At a nod from the captain, Lieutenant Larson reached up and shut off the motor. The sudden silence was startling.

Dick understood what was to be done. They were to glide, or as it is called "volplane" (pronounced vol-pla-nay, with the accent on the last syllable) to the ground.

"I hope we make it safely," mused Dick. But it did not look as though they had been near enough the landing place when the motor was cut off. Dick saw the two army men glance rather apprehensively at one another. Was something wrong?

Dick was sure of it a moment later when, as Captain Grantly pulled the lever of the deflecting rudder toward him, there was a snapping, breaking sound.

"Lost control!" cried the captain. "Wire snapped! Look out, everybody!"

Dick wanted to jump, but he knew that would be rash, as they were still some distance above the ground.

"Can't you guide her?" asked Larson.

"No! We've got to land the best we can!" was the answer.

They were right over a little farm now, and seemed to be headed directly for a small, low building.

"Something is going to smash!" thought Dick grimly.

The next moment the airship had come down on the roof of the low farm building, crashing right through it, and a second later Dick and his companions found themselves in the midst of a squealing lot of pigs, that fairly rushed over them.

CHAPTER VIII

AT HAMILTON CORNERS

Instinctively, as he felt the airship falling, without being under control, Dick had loosed the strap that held him to his seat. This advice had been given as one of the first instructions, to enable the aviator to leap clear of the craft as it struck.

But, in this case the landing had been such a queer one that there was no time for any of the three to do the latter. Down on the roof of the pig sty they had come, crashing through it, for the place was old and rotten.

It was this very fact, however, that saved them from more serious injuries than severe joltings. The roof had collapsed, had broken in the middle, and the squealing porkers were now running wild. Most of them seemed to prefer the vicinity of the spot near where the three aviators were now tumbled in a heap, having been thus thrown by the concussion.

"Get out of here, you razor-back!" cried Dick, as a pig fairly walked over him. He managed to struggle to his feet, but another pig took that, seemingly, as an invitation to dart between the legs of the young millionaire, and upset him.

Dick fell directly back on the form of Captain Grantly, who grunted at the impact. Then, as Lieutenant Larson tried to get up, he, too, was bowled over by a rush of some more pigs.

But the two army officers, and Dick, were football players, and they knew how to take a fall, so were not harmed. Fortunately they had been tossed out on a grassy part of the pen, and away from the muddy slough where the porkers were in the habit of wallowing.

"Get out, you brutes!" cried Dick, striking at the pigs with a part of one of the pen roof boards. Then, with the army men to help him, he succeeded in driving the swine out of their way. This done, the aviators looked at one another and "took an account of stock."

"Are you hurt?" asked the captain of Dick, grimly.

"No, only bruised a bit. As the old lady said of the train that came to a sudden halt because of a collision, 'do you always land this way?'"

"No, indeed!" exclaimed the captain, as he looked at the ruin of the shed, amid which the airship was. "This is my first accident of this kind. The lever of the vertical rudder snapped, and I couldn't control her. Luckily the roof was rotten, or we might have smashed everything."

"As it is, nothing seems to be much damaged," said the lieutenant. "I wonder if we can fly back?"

"It is doubtful," the captain answered. "We'll try and get her out, first."

As they were climbing over the pile of broken boards to get a view of the aeroplane, an excited farmer came rushing out of a barn, a short distance away.

"Hey, what do you fellers mean—smashing down out of the clouds, bustin' up my pig pen, and scatterin' 'em to the four winds?" he yelled. "I'll have th' law on you for this! I'll make you pay damages! You killed a lot of my pigs, I reckon!"

"I don't see any dead ones," spoke the captain, calmly. "It was an accident."

"That's what them autermobile fellers says when they run over my chickens," snarled the unpleasant farmer. "But they has t' pay for 'em all the same."

"And we are willing to pay you anything in reason," said the Captain. "I don't believe we killed any of your pigs, however. But the shed was so rotten it was ready to fall down of itself, which was a good thing for us. How much do you want?"

"Well, I want a hundred dollars—that's what I want."

"The shed, when new, wasn't worth a quarter of that."

"I don't care!" snapped the farmer. "That's my price. Some of my pigs may be lost for all I know, and pork's goin' t' be high this year. I want a hundred dollars, or you don't take your old shebang offen my premises. I'll hold it till you pay me."

The army officers looked serious at this. Clearly the farmer had a right to damages, but a hundred dollars was excessive.

"I'll give you fifty, cash," said Dick, as he pulled out a roll of bills. "Will that satisfy you?"

The farmer's eyes gleamed at the sight of the money. And, as Dick looked at his companions, he caught a greedy glint in the eyes of Lieutenant Larson.

"It's wuth a hundred; smashin' my shed, an' all the trouble you've caused me," grumbled the farmer. "But I'll take sixty."

"No you won't. You'll take fifty or you can bring a lawsuit," replied Dick, sharply. "I guess you know who I am. I'm Hamilton, from the Kentfield Academy. Colonel Masterly buys some garden stuff of you, and if I tell him—"

"Oh, shucks, give me the fifty!" cried the farmer, eagerly, as he held out his hand for the money. "And don't you try any more tricks like that ag'in!"

"We haven't any desire to," said Captain Grantly. "Now we'll see if we can navigate."

"And I've got t' see if I kin get them pigs together," grumbled the farmer, as he pocketed Dick's money.

"You can put in a requisition for this, I suppose," suggested the lieutenant. "I don't know whether Uncle Sam ought to reimburse you, or we, personally."

"Don't mention it!" exclaimed Dick. "I'm always willing to pay for damages, though I suppose if my Uncle Ezra Larabee was here he'd haggle with that farmer and make him throw in a pig or two for luck."

"Who is Uncle Ezra Larabee?" asked the lieutenant, curiously.

"A relative of mine," answered Dick. "Rather 'close' as regards money."

"Is he rich?"

"Yes, quite wealthy, but you'd never know it. He lives in Dankville, and he and my dog Grit never can get along together. He hates Grit and I guess Grit doesn't love him. But shall we try to get this machine out of the shed?"

"I guess it's the best thing to do, now that the pigs are out of the way," agreed the captain.

And, while the farmer and his hired man were chasing after the escaped pigs, the army officers and Dick began extricating the airship. The splintered boards of the pig-shed were pulled to one side, and then it was seen that, aside from a broken landing wheel, little damage had been done. The engine was not harmed in the least and the snapped wire that had prevented the rudder being set to make a proper landing, was easy to splice.

"And, as we've got a spare wheel we can put that on and soon start back," said the lieutenant.

"Say, this is getting off better than even in an automobile accident," spoke Dick, with a laugh. "I didn't know you carried spare parts."

"We do the wheels, as they are very light," the captain said. "Now let's roll her out and see what we can do."

The smashed wheel was removed from the axle, and the spare one substituted. The broken wire was repaired and the aeroplane was now about the same as before. It was rolled to a level place, and the motor tested. It ran perfectly.

The farmer, having collected all his pigs, and perhaps feeling joyful because of the fifty dollars in his pocket, agreed to "hold back" on the craft, to steady it until the necessary speed of the motor had been attained. His hired man helped him.

Just as the captain was about to give the word to "let go" the other airship was seen coming to look for the missing one. But there was now no need of assistance, and, a moment later, Dick and his companions again arose in the air.

A quick return was made to the Academy, those in the other airship being informed, by a signal, that all was now right. When the story of the queer landing was told, Dick was regarded as a hero by his companions.

"Just think!" complained Paul, whimsically, "your first trip, and you have an accident and you don't get so much as a scratch."

"Yes, but I got run over and knocked down by a pig," laughed Dick. "I'll take the scratches, please. No more pigs!"

"And after that, are you still going to build an airship?" asked Innis.

"I sure am! It's the greatest sensation in the world—aviation! I wouldn't miss it for a fortune. And I'm going to pull down that twenty thousand dollar prize; don't forget that, fellows."

"Good luck!" wished Paul.

In the days that followed there were many more airship flights, but no accidents of moment. Dick went up again several times, and at last was allowed to run the aeroplane himself, with the captain and lieutenant to coach him. Then only one officer went along, another cadet being taken up with Dick.

And finally the day came when Dick was qualified to take the craft up alone, with two other cadets. He had graduated as a pilot of the air, and properly proud he was of the honor.

"All you want now is experience," said Captain Grantly, as Dick came back after a successful flight with Paul and Innis. "And that takes time."

Dick's two intimate chums also qualified as amateur pilots, and a number of other cadets were equally successful. The aviation course at Kentfield was very popular.

Then came the end of the term, and the summer vacation was at hand. The last drills and guard-mounts were held. The graduation exercises were finished in a "blaze of glory." The Juniors gave a gay dance, at which Dick and his chums met the pretty girls whom they had seen at the dock that day.

"And now for Hamilton Corners!" cried the young millionaire, when the Academy was formally closed for the term. "I want you fellows to come out with me, and watch my airship being built."

Mr. Vardon had found he could not build for Dick at Kentfield the craft he wanted. It would take too long, and there were not the facilities. So he and his helper went to Hamilton Corners, to do the preliminary work. Dick and his chums were to follow as soon as school was over. Larry Dexter went back to New York, but promised to join Dick in time for the flight for the big government prize.

"Well, Dad, how are you?" cried Dick, as he greeted his father at the family mansion in Hamilton Corners.

"Fine, my boy! There's no use asking how YOU are, I can see you are fine!"

"Did Vardon and Jack get here? Have they started work?" Dick wanted to know.

"Yes, I did just as you asked me to in your letter. I let them have the run of the place, and they've been busy ever since they came. I hope you are successful, Dick, but, I have my doubts."

"I'll show you!" cried the cadet enthusiastically.

CHAPTER IX

UNCLE EZRA'S VISIT

Dick and his father had much to talk about concerning the airship. Dick explained his plans, and described the new stabilizer.

"Well, now that you have explained it to me, I don't see but what it may be possible," said Mr. Hamilton, after carefully considering the matter. "It isn't so much the expense, since you have your own fortune, but, of course, there is the element of danger to be considered."

"Well, there's danger in anything," agreed Dick. "But I think I have a lucky streak in me,—after the way we came out of that pig-pen accident," and he laughed.

"Yes, you were fortunate," conceded Mr. Hamilton. "But, don't take too many risks, my son. Go in and win, if you can, but don't be rash. I am still from Missouri, and you've got to show me. Now I've got a lot of business to attend to, and so I'll have to leave you to your own devices. You say Paul and Innis are coming on?"

"Yes, they'll be here in a few days and stay until the airship is completed. Then they'll fly with me."

"Anybody else going?"

"Yes, Larry Dexter—you remember him?"

"Oh, sure! The young reporter."

"And I think I'll take Mr. Vardon along. We may need his help in an emergency."

"A good idea. Well, I wish you luck!"

A large barn on the Hamilton property had been set aside for the use of the aviator and his men, for he had engaged several more besides Jack Butt to hurry along the work on Dick's new aircraft. The order had been placed for the motor, and that, it was promised, would be ready in time.

Dick, having had lunch, went out to see how his airship was progressing. Grit raced here and there, glad to be back home again, though he would probably miss the many horses and grooms at Kentfield. For Grit loved to be around the stables, and the hostlers made much of him.

"How are you coming on?" asked the young millionaire, as he surveyed the framework of the big craft that, he hoped, would carry him across the continent and win for him the twenty thousand dollar prize.

"Fine, Dick!" exclaimed Mr. Vardon. "Everything is working out well. Come in and look. You can get an idea of the machine now."

Dick Hamilton's airship was radically different from any craft previously built, yet fundamentally, it was on the same principle as a biplane. But it was more than three times as large as the average biplane, and was built in two sections.

That is there were four sets of double planes, or eight in all, and between them was an enclosed cabin containing the motor, the various controls, places to sleep and eat, the cabin also forming the storage room for the oil, gasolene and other supplies.

This cabin was not yet built, but, as I have said, it would be "amidship" if one may use that term concerning an airship. Thus the occupants would be protected from the elements, and could move about in comfort, not being obliged to sit rigidly in a seat for hours at a time.

"She's going to be pretty big," remarked Dick, as he walked about the skeleton of his new craft.

"She has to be able to carry all you want to take in her," said the aviator. "But she'll be speedy for all of that, for the engine will be very powerful."

"Will she be safe?" asked Dick.

"As safe as any airship. I am going to incorporate in her my gyroscope equilibrizer, or stabilizer, as you suggested."

"Oh, yes, I want that!" said Dick, in a decided tone.

"It is very good of you to allow me to demonstrate my patent on your craft," the inventor said. "It will be a fine thing for me if you win the prize, and it is known that my stabilizer was aboard to aid you," he said, with shining, eager eyes.

"Well, I'm only too glad I can help you in that small way," spoke Dick. "I'm sure your patent is a valuable one."

"And I am now positive that it will work properly," went on Mr. Vardon.

"And I'll take precious good care that no sneak, like Larson, gets a chance to tamper with it!" exclaimed Jack Butt.

"You must not make such positive statements," warned his chief. "It may not have been Larson."

"Well, your machine was tampered with; wasn't it, just before we sank into the river?"

"Yes, and that was what made us fall."

"Well, I'm sure Larson monkeyed with it, and no one can make me believe anything else," said Jack, positively. "If he comes around here—"

"He isn't likely to," interrupted Dick. "The army aviators were sent to Texas, I believe, to give some demonstrations at a post there."

"You never can tell where Larson will turn up," murmured Jack.

Dick was shown the progress of the work, and was consulted about several small changes from the original, tentative plans. He agreed to them, and then, as it was only a question of waiting until his craft was done, he decided to call on some of his friends at Hamilton Corners.

Innis and Paul arrived in due season, and were delighted at the sight of Dick's big, new aircraft, which, by the time they saw it, had assumed more definite shape. Mr. Vardon and his men had worked rapidly.

"And that cabin is where we'll stay; is that it?" asked Paul, as he looked at the framework.

"That's to be our quarters," answered the young millionaire.

Paul was looking carefully on all sides of it.

"Something missing?" asked Dick, noting his chum's anxiety.

"I was looking for the fire escape."

"Fire escape!" cried Dick. "What in the world would you do with a fire escape on an airship?"

"Well, you're going to carry a lot of gasolene, you say. If that gets afire we'll want to escape; won't we? I suggest a sort of rope ladder, that can be uncoiled and let down to the ground. That might answer."

"Oh, slosh!" cried Dick. "There's going to be no fire aboard the—say, fellows, I haven't named her yet! I wonder what I'd better call her?

"Call her the Abaris," suggested Innis, "though he wasn't a lady."

"Who was he?" asked Dick. "That name sounds well."

"Abaris, if you will look in the back of your dictionary, you will note was a Scythian priest of Apollo," said Innis, with a patronizing air at his display of knowledge. "He is said to have ridden through the air on an arrow. Isn't that a good name for your craft, Dick?"

"It sure is. I'll christen her Abaris as soon as she's ready to launch. Good idea, Innis."

"Oh, I'm full of 'em," boasted the cadet, strutting about.

"You're full of conceit—that's what you are," laughed Paul.

Suddenly there came a menacing growl from Grit, who was outside the airship shed, and Dick called a warning.

"Who's there?" he asked, thinking it might be a stranger.

A rasping voice answered:

"It's me! Are you there, Nephew Richard? I went all through the house, but nobody seemed to be home."

"It's Uncle Ezra!" whispered Dick, making a pretense to faint.

"I've come to pay you a little visit," went on the crabbed old miser. "Where's your pa?"

"Why, he's gone to New York."

"Ha! Another sinful and useless waste of money! I never did see the beat!"

"He had to go, on business," answered Dick.

"Humph! Couldn't he write? A two cent stamp is a heap sight cheaper than an excursion ticket to New York. But Mortimer never did know the value of money," sighed Uncle Ezra.

Grit growled again.

"Nephew Richard, if your dog bites me I'll make you pay the doctor bills," warned Mr. Ezra Larabee.

"Here, Grit! Quiet!" cried Dick, and the animal came inside, looking very much disgusted.

Uncle Ezra looked in at the door of the shed, and saw the outlines of the airship.

"What foolishness is this?" he asked, seeming to take it for granted that all Dick did was foolish.

"It's my new airship," answered the young millionaire.

"An airship! Nephew Richard Hamilton! Do you mean to tell me that you are sinfully wasting money on such a thing as that—on something that will never go, and will only be a heap of junk?" and Uncle Ezra, of Dankville, looked as though his nephew were a fit subject for a lunatic asylum.

CHAPTER X

BUILDING THE AIRSHIP

Grit growled in a deep, threatening voice, and Uncle Ezra looked around with startled suddenness.

"I guess I'd better chain him up before I answer you," said Dick, grimly. "Here, old boy!"

The bulldog came, unwillingly enough, and was made secure.

"An—an airship!" gasped Uncle Ezra, as though he could not believe it. "An airship, Nephew Richard. It will never go. You might a good deal better take the money that you are so foolishly wasting, and put it in a savings bank. Or, I would sell you some stock in my woolen mill. That would pay you four per cent, at least."

"But my airship is going to go," declared the young millionaire. "It's on the same model as one I've ridden in, and it's going to go. We're sure of it; aren't we, Mr. Vardon?"

"Oh, it will GO all right," declared the aviator. "I'm sure of that. But I don't guarantee that you'll win the prize money."

"What's that? What's that?" asked Uncle Ezra in surprise. He was all attention when it came to a matter of money. "What prize did you speak of?"

"Didn't you hear, Uncle Ezra?" inquired Dick. "Why, the United States government, to increase the interest in aviation, and to encourage inventors, has offered a prize of twenty thousand dollars to the first person who takes his airship from the Atlantic to the Pacific, or rather, from New York to San Francisco with but two landings. I'm going to have a try for that prize!"

"Yes, and he's going to win it, too!" cried Paul.

"And we're at least going to share in the glory of it," added Innis.

"Twenty thousand dollars!" murmured Uncle Ezra. "Is it possible?"

"Oh, it's true enough, sir," put in Mr. Vardon. "The offer has been formally made. I know several of my aviator friends who are going to have a try for it. I intended to myself, but for the accident in which my craft was smashed. Only for the kindness of your nephew in engaging me on this work I don't know what I should be doing now."

"That's all right!" interrupted Dick, who disliked praise. "I'm doing MYSELF as much a favor in having you build this airship as I am YOU. I intend to have a good time in this craft, even if I don't win the prize."

"Twenty thousand dollars," murmured Uncle Ezra again, slowly. "It's an awful lot of money—an awful lot," he added in an awed tone of voice.

The truth of the matter was that Uncle Ezra had nearly a million. But he was very "close," and never missed a chance to make more.

"And do you intend to get the government prize in that—that contraption?" he asked, motioning to the half-completed aeroplane.

"Oh, it isn't finished yet," explained Dick.

"When it is, it will be one of the finest aircraft in this, or any other, country," declared Mr. Vardon. "I don't say that just because I am building it, but because Mr. Hamilton is putting into it the very best materials that can be bought."

"And we mustn't forget your stabilizer," laughed Dick.

"What's that?" Uncle Ezra wanted to know. Since hearing about the twenty thousand dollar prize his interest in airships seemed to have increased.

"The stabilizer, or equalibrizer, whatever you wish to call it, is to keep the airship from turning over," explained Mr. Vardon, and he went into the details with which I have already acquainted my readers.

But it is doubtful if Uncle Ezra heard, or at least he paid little attention, for he was murmuring over and over again to himself:

"Twenty thousand dollars! Twenty thousand dollars! That's an awful lot of money. I—I'd like to get it myself."

From time to time Grit growled, and finally Uncle Ezra, perhaps fearing that the dog might get loose and bite him, said:

"I think I'll go in the house for a while, Nephew Richard. Your father is not likely to be home today, but as I have missed the last train back to Dankville, listening to your talk about airships—foolish talk it seems to me—I will have to stay all night."

"Oh, certainly!" exclaimed Dick, remembering that he must play the host. "Go right in, Uncle Ezra and tell the butler to get you a lunch. I'll be in immediately."

"Well, I could eat a little snack," admitted the crabbed old man. "I did think of stopping in the restaurant at the railroad depot on my way here, and getting a sandwich. But the girl said sandwiches were ten cents, and they didn't look worth it to me.

"I asked her if she didn't have some made with stale bread, that she could let me have for five cents, but she said they didn't sell stale sandwiches. She seemed real put-out about it, too. She needn't have. Stale bread's better for you than fresh, anyhow.

"But I didn't buy one. I wasn't going to throw away ten cents. That's the interest money on a dollar for two whole years."

Then he started back to the house.

"Isn't he the limit!" cried Dick, in despair. "He's got almost as much money as we have, and he's so afraid of spending a cent that he actually goes hungry, I believe. And his house—why he's got a fine one, but the only rooms he and Aunt Samantha ever open are the kitchen and one bedroom. I had to spend some time there once, as I guess you fellows know, and say—good-night!" cried Dick, with a tragic gesture.

"He seemed interested in airships," ventured Paul.

"It was the twenty thousand dollars he was interested in," laughed Dick. "I wonder if he—"

"What?" asked Innis, as the young millionaire paused.

"Oh, nothing," was the answer. "I just thought of something, but it's too preposterous to mention. Say, Mr. Vardon, when do you expect our engine?"

"Oh, in about a week now. I won't be ready for it before then. We can give it a try-out on the blocks before we mount it, to see if it develops enough speed and power. But have you made your official entry for the prize yet?"

"No, and I think I'd better," Dick said. "I'll do it at once."

Dick and his chums had their lunch, and then went for a ride in Dick's motor-boat, which had been brought on from Kentfield. They had a jolly time, and later in the afternoon returned to watch the construction of the airship.

The building of the Abaris, as Dick had decided to call his craft, went on apace during the days that followed. Uncle Ezra was more interested than Dick had believed possible, and prolonged his stay nearly a week. He paid many visits to the airship shed.

Mr. Vardon, and Jack, his right-hand man, and the other workmen labored hard. The airship began to look like what she was intended for. She was of a new model and shape, and seemed to be just what Dick wanted. Of course she was in a sense an experiment.

The main cabin, though, containing the living and sleeping quarters, as well as the machinery, was what most pleased Dick and his chums.

"It's like traveling in a first-class motor-boat, only up in the clouds, instead of in the water," declared Innis.

CHAPTER XI

A SURPRISE

"Toss over that monkey wrench; will you?"

"Say, who had the saw last?"

"I know I laid a hammer down here, but it's gone now!"

"Look out there! Low bridge! Gangway! One side!"

These, and many other cries and calls, came from the big barn-like shed, where Dick Hamilton's airship was being constructed. Dick himself, and his two chums, Innis Beeby and Paul Drew, had joined forces with Mr. Vardon in helping on the completion of the Abaris.

"We've got to get a move on!" Dick had said, after he had sent in his application to compete for the twenty thousand dollar government prize. "We don't want to be held back at the last minute. Boys, we've got to work on this airship ourselves."

"We're with you!" cried Innis and Paul, eagerly.

And so, after some preliminary instructions from Mr. Vardon, the cadets had taken the tools and started to work.

It did not come so unhandily to them as might have been imagined. At the Kentfield Military Academy they had been called upon to do much manual labor, in preparation for a military life.

There had been pontoon bridges to build across streams, by means of floats and boats. There had been other bridges to throw across defiles and chasms. There were artillery and baggage wagons to transport along poor roads. And all this, done for practice, now stood Dick and his chums in good stead.

They knew how to employ their hands, which is the best training in the world for a young man, and they could also use tools to advantage.

So now we find Dick, Paul and Innis laboring over the new airship, in which the young millionaire hoped to make a flight across the United States, from ocean to ocean.

"That's what I like to see!" exclaimed Uncle Ezra, as he came out to the shed just before he started back for Dankville. "It does young men good to work. Pity more of 'em don't do it. Hard work and plain food is what the rising generation wants. I don't approve of airships—that is as a rule," the crabbed old miser hastily added, "but, of course, twenty thousand dollars is a nice prize to win. I only hope you get it. Nephew Richard. I like to see you work. I'm going back now. I'll tell your Aunt Samantha that you've at last learned how to do something, even if it is only building an airship."

"Don't you call my studies at Kentfield something, Uncle Ezra?" asked Dick.

"No sir! No, sir-ee!" cried the elderly man. "That's time and money thrown away. But I see that you can do manual labor, Nephew Richard, and if you really want to do useful work, and earn money, I'd be glad to have you in my woolen mill. I could start you on three dollars and a half a week, and you could soon earn more. Will you come?"

"No, thank you," said Dick. "Thank you just the same."

He had a vivid idea of what it might mean to work for his Uncle Ezra. Besides, Dick's fortune was such that he did not have to work. But he fully intended to, and he was getting a training that would enable him to work to the best advantage. Just because he was a millionaire he did not despise work. In fact he liked it, and he had made up his mind that he would not be an idler.

Just now aviation attracted him, and he put in as many hours working over his airship—hard work, too,—as many a mechanic might have done.

"Well, I'll say good-bye, Nephew Richard," spoke Uncle Ezra, after walking about the big airship, and looking at it more closely than would seem natural, after he had characterized it as a "foolish piece of business."

"I'm sorry you won't stay until my father gets back," spoke Dick. "I expect him tomorrow, or next day."

"Well, if I stayed I know my hired man would waste a lot of feed on the horses," said Uncle Ezra. "And every time I go away he sits up and burns his kerosene lamp until almost ten o'clock at night. And oil has gone up something terrible of late."

"Well, I hope you'll come and see us again," invited Dick, as his uncle started to go. "But won't you let me send you to the station in the auto? It isn't being used."

"No, Nephew Richard. Not for me!" exclaimed Uncle Ezra. "You might bust a tire, and then you'd expect me to pay for it."

"Oh, no, I wouldn't!"

"Well, then, there might be some accident, and I might get my clothes torn. That would mean I'd have to have a new suit. I've worn this one five years, and it's good for three more, if I'm careful of it!" he boasted, as he looked down at his shiny, black garments.

"Then you're going to walk?" asked Dick.

"Yes, Nephew Richard. There's grass almost all the way to the station, and I can keep on that. It will save my shoes."

"But people don't like you to walk on their grass," objected Dick.

"Huh! Think I'm going to tramp on the hard sidewalks and wear out my shoe leather?" cried Uncle Ezra. "I guess not!"

He started off, trudging along with his cane, but paused long enough to call back:

"Oh, Nephew Richard, I got the cook to put me up some sandwiches. I can eat them on the train, and save buying. The idea of charging ten cents in the railroad restaurant! It's robbery! I had her use stale bread, so that won't be wasted."

Dick hopelessly shook his head. He really could say nothing.

His chums knew Uncle Ezra's character, and sympathized with their friend.

The cadets resumed work on the big airship. The framework of the wings had been completed, and all that was necessary was to stretch on the specially made canvas. The cabin was nearing completion, and the place for the engine had been built. The big propellers had been constructed of several layers of mahogany, and tested at a speed to which they would never be subjected in a flight. The bicycle wheels on which the big airship would run along the ground, until it had acquired momentum for a rise, were put in place.

"I didn't just like those hydroplanes, though," said Dick, who had added them as an after thought. "I think they should be made larger."

"And I agree with you," said Mr. Vardon. "The only use you will have for the hydroplanes, or wheel-pontoons, will be in case you are compelled to make a landing on the water. But they should be larger, or you will not float sufficiently high. Make them larger. But it will cost more money."

"I don't mind that," returned Dick. "Of course I am not anxious to throw money away, but I want to make a success of this, and win the prize, not so much because of the cash, as to show how your equilibrizer works, and to prove that it is possible to make an airship flight across the continent.

"So, if bigger hydroplanes are going to make it more certain for us to survive an accident, put them on."

"I will," promised the aviator.

Pontoons, or hydroplanes, in this case, I might state, were hollow, water-tight, wooden boxes, so fitted near the wheels of the airship, that they could be lowered by levers in case the craft had to descend on water. They were designed to support her on the waves.

Several days of hard work passed. The aircraft was nearing completion. The cabin was finished, and had been fitted up with most of the apparatus and the conveniences for the trip. There were instruments to tell how fast the Abaris was traveling, how far she was above the earth, the speed and direction of the wind and machinery, and others, to predict, as nearly as possible, future weather conditions.

In the front of the cabin was a small pilothouse, in which the operator would have his place. From there he could guide the craft, and control it in every possible way.

There was a sleeping cabin, fitted with bunks, a combined kitchen and dining-room, a small living-room, and the motor-room. Of course the latter took up the most space, being the most important.

In addition there was an outside platform, built in the rear of the enclosed cabin, where one could stand and look above the clouds, or at the earth below.

Gasolene and storage batteries furnished the power, and there was plenty in reserve. Dick wanted to take no chances in his prize flight.

The second day after Uncle Ezra's departure the motor for the airship arrived.

"Now for a test!" cried Dick, when the machine had been uncrated and set up on the temporary base. The attachments were made, an extra pair of trial propellers connected, and the power turned on.

With a roar and a throb, the motor started, and as Mr. Vardon glanced at the test gages with anxious eyes he cried:

"She does better than we expected, Dick! We can cross the continent with that engine, and not have to make more than two stops."

"Are you sure?" asked the young millionaire.

"Positive," was the answer.

Further tests confirmed this opinion, and preparations were made to install the motor in the airship.

It was while this was being done that a servant brought Dick a message.

"Someone has called to see you," said the man.

"Who is it?"

"He says his name is Lieutenant Larson, formerly of the United States Army, and he has important information for you."

"Larson!" exclaimed Dick in surprise. "I wonder what he wants of me?"

"Will you see him?" asked Paul.

"I suppose I had better," said Dick, slowly. "I wonder what he wants?"

CHAPTER XII

LARSON SEES UNCLE EZRA

Dick Hamilton had not been very friendly with Lieutenant Larson during the aviation instruction at Kentfield. In fact the young millionaire did not like the army officer. Added to this the suspicion that Larson might have had some hand in tampering with the stabilizer of Mr. Vardon's craft, did not make Dick any too anxious to see the birdman.

And yet he felt that in courtesy he must.

"I'll go in the library and meet him," said Dick, to the servant who had brought the message. "I don't care to have him out here, where he might see my airship," Dick added, to his chums.

"I guess you're right there," agreed Paul.

"He might take some of your ideas, and make a machine for himself that would win the prize," added Innis.

"Oh, well, I'm not so afraid of that," replied Dick, "as I intend, after I complete my craft, and if she wins the prize, to turn my plans and ideas over to the government, anyhow, for their use. But I don't just like the idea of Larson coming out to the work-shed."

Mr. Vardon and his men were in another part of the big barn, and had not heard of the arrival of the army man.

"How do you do?" greeted Dick, as he met Larson in the library. "I'm glad to see you."

This was polite fiction, that, perhaps, might be pardoned.

"I don't want to trouble you, Mr. Hamilton," went on the lieutenant, with a shifty glance around the room, "but I have left the army, and have engaged in the building of airships.

"I recall that you said at Kentfield, that you were going to construct one, and I called to see if I could not get the contract," Larson went on.

"Well, I am sorry, for your sake, to say that my craft is almost completed," replied Dick. "So I can't give you the contract."

"Completed!" cried Larson, in tones that showed his great surprise. "You don't mean to tell me you have undertaken the important work of constructing an aeroplane so soon after coming from the military academy?"

"Well, I didn't want to waste any time," replied Dick, wondering at the lieutenant's interest. "I'm going to try for the government prize, and I wanted to be early on the job."

Larson hesitated a moment, and resumed:

"Well, then it is too late; I suppose? I hoped to get you to adopt my plans for an aeroplane. But I have been delayed making arrangements, and by resigning from the army.

"Perhaps I am not too late, though, to have you adopt my type of equilibrizer. My mercury tubes—"

"I am sorry, but you are too late there," interrupted Dick.

"What type are you using?" the lieutenant cried, dramatically.

"The Vardon. I might say that Mr. Vardon is also building my airship. It will contain his gyroscope."

"A gyroscope!" cried the former officer. "You are very foolish! You will come to grief with that. The only safe form is the mercury tube, of which I am the inventor."

At that moment Vardon himself, who wished to consult Dick on some point, came into the room, not knowing a caller was there.

"I am sorry," went on the young millionaire, "but I am going to use Mr. Vardon's gyroscope."

"Then you may as well give up all hope of winning the prize!" sneered Larson. "You are a very foolish young man. Vardon is a dreamer, a visionary inventor who will never amount to anything. His gyroscope is a joke, and—"

"I am sorry you think so," interrupted the aviator. "But you evidently considered my gyroscope such a good joke that you tried to spoil it."

"I! What do you mean? You shall answer for that!" cried the former lieutenant, in an unnecessarily dramatic manner.

"I think you know what I mean," replied Vardon, coolly. "I need not go into details. Only I warn you that if you are seen tampering about the Hamilton airship, on which I am working, that you will not get off so easily as you did in my case!"

"Be careful!" warned Larson. "You are treading on dangerous ground!"

"And so are you," warned the aviator, not allowing himself to get excited as did Larson. "I know of what I am speaking."

"Then I want to tell you that you are laboring under a misapprehension," sneered the former officer. "I can see that I am not welcome here. I'll go."

Dick did not ask him to stay. The young millionaire was anything but a hypocrite.

"What did he want?" asked Mr. Vardon, when Larson had left.

"To build my airship. He evidently did not know that I had already engaged you. He got a surprise, I think."

"He is a dangerous man, and an unscrupulous one," said the aviator. "I do not say that through any malice, but because I firmly believe it. I would never trust him."

"Nor shall I," added Dick. "I presume though, that he will have some feeling against me for this."

"Very likely," agreed Mr. Vardon. "You will have to be on your guard."

The young millionaire and the aviator then went into details about some complicated point in the construction of the Abaris, with which it is not necessary to weary my readers.

Larson must have recalled what Dick had told him about Uncle Ezra being a wealthy man, for, as subsequent events disclosed, the disappointed army officer went almost at once to Dankville. And there he laid before the miserly man a plan which Uncle Ezra eventually took up, strange as it may seen.

It was the bait of the twenty thousand dollar prize that "took," in his case.

Larson had some trouble in reaching Mr. Larabee, who was a bit shy of strangers. When one, (in this case Larson) was announced by Aunt Samantha, Mr. Larabee asked:

"Does he look like an agent?"

"No, Ez, I can't say he does."

"Does he look like a collector?"

"No, Ez, not the usual kind."

"Or a missionary, looking for funds to buy pocket handkerchiefs for the heathen?"

"Hardly. He's smoking, and I wish you'd hurry and git him out of the parlor, for he's sure to drop some ashes on the carpet that we've had ever since we got married."

"Smoking in my parlor!" exclaimed Uncle Ezra. "I'll get him out of there. The idea! Why, if any sun is let in there it will spoil the colors. How'd you come to open that?" he asked of his wife, wrathfully.

"I didn't. But I was so surprised at havin' someone come to the front door, which they never do, that I didn't know what to say. He asked if you was to home, and I said you was. Then he said: 'Well, I'll wait for him in here,' and he pushed open the parlor door and went in. I had it open the least mite, for I thought I saw a speck of sun comin' through a crack in the blinds and I was goin' in to close it when the bell rang."

"The idea! Sitting in my parlor!" muttered Uncle Ezra. "I'll get him out of that. You're sure he ain't a book peddler?"

"He don't seem to have a thing to sell except nerve," said Aunt Samantha, "and he sure has got plenty of that."

"I'll fix him!" cried Uncle Ezra.

But he proved to be no match for the smooth sharper in the shape of Larson.

"Did you want to see me?" demanded the crabbed old man.

"I did," answered Larson coolly, as he continued to puff away at his cigar. "I came to offer you a chance to make twenty thousand dollars."

"Twenty thousand dollars!" Uncle Ezra nearly lost his breath, he was so surprised.

"That's what I said! I'm in a position to give you a good chance to make that much money, and perhaps more. If you will give me half an hour of your time—"

"Look here!" interrupted Mr. Larabee, "this ain't no lottery scheme; is it? If it is I want to warn you that I'm a deacon in the church. I wouldn't go into any lottery unless

I was sure I could win. I don't believe in gambling. As a deacon of the church I couldn't countenance nothing like that. No gambling!"

"This is not a gamble," Larson assured him. "It's a sure thing. I'll show you how to make twenty thousand dollars!"

"I—I guess I'd better open a window in here, so we can see," said Uncle Ezra, faintly. "That's quite a pile of money to talk about in the dark," and to the horror of Aunt Samantha she saw, a little later, the sun shamelessly streaming in on her carpet that had only been treated to such indignities on the occasions of a funeral, or something like that. The parlor of the Dankville house was like a tomb in this respect.

CHAPTER XIII

UNCLE EZRA ACTS QUEERLY

Exactly what passed between Uncle Ezra Larabee and his caller, Aunt Samantha never learned. She was so overcome at seeing the parlor opened, that perhaps she did not listen sufficiently careful. She overheard the murmur of voices, and, now and then, such expressions as "above the clouds," "in the air," "twenty thousand dollars, and maybe more."

"Gracious goodness!" she murmured as she hurried out to the kitchen, where she smelled something burning on the stove. "I wonder what it's all about? Can Ezra have lost money on some of his investments? If he has, if it's gone up above the clouds, and in the air, the way he's talking about it things will be terrible; terrible! It will come nigh onto killin' him, I expect!"

She went back to listen again outside the parlor door, but could make out nothing.

She did catch, however, her husband's expression of:

"Twenty thousand dollars! It's a pile of money! A heap!"

"Oh my!" she murmured faintly. "If he's lost that we'll go to the poorhouse, sure!"

But nothing like that happened. As a matter of fact Uncle Ezra could have lost that sum several times over, and not have felt it except in the anguish of his mind.

When the caller had gone, Uncle Ezra seemed rather cheerful, much to the amazement of Aunt Samantha. She could not understand it. At the same time her husband appeared to be worried about something.

"But he doesn't act as though he had lost a lot of money," his wife reasoned. "He certainly acts queer, but not just that way. I wonder what it can be?"

And during the next week Uncle Ezra acted more queerly than ever. He received several other visits from the strange man who had given his name to Aunt Samantha, when first calling, as "Lieutenant Larson." Also, Mr. Larabee went off on several short trips.

"I wonder whatever's got into him?" mused Aunt Samantha. "I never knew him to act this way before. I do hope he isn't doing anything rash!"

If she had only known!

Uncle Ezra became more and more engrossed with his caller who came several days in succession. They were shut up together in the parlor, and one window shutter was opened each time, to the horror of Mrs. Larabee.

"That carpet will be faded all out, and clean ruined," she complained to her husband.

"Well, if it is, maybe I'll get money enough to buy a new one," said Uncle Ezra. "Mind, I'm not saying for sure," he added, cautiously, "but maybe."

"Why, how you talk!" cried Aunt Samantha. "That carpet ought to last us until we die! A new carpet! I never heard tell of such a thing! Never in all my born days! The idea!"

Uncle Ezra chuckled grimly. It was clear that he was acting in a new role, and he was a surprise, even to himself.

At last Aunt Samantha could stand the suspense no longer. One night, after a rather restless period, she awakened Uncle Ezra who had, most unusually, been talking in his sleep.

"Ezra! Ezra! Wake up!" she demanded in a loud whisper, at the same time vigorously shaking him.

"Eh! What is it? Burglars?" he asked, sitting up in bed.

"No, Ezra. Nothin' like that!"

"Oh, cats, eh? Well, if it's only cats go to sleep. I don't mind 'em."

"No, Ezra, I didn't say cats. But you're talkin' in your sleep. That is, you were."

"I was?"

"Yes."

"What'd I say?" and he seemed anxious.

"Why you were talkin' a lot about flyin' in the air, and goin' up to the clouds, and bein' in a race, and winnin' twenty thousand dollars! Oh, Ezra, if you care for me at all, tell me what mystery this is!" she pleaded.

"Did I say all that?" he asked, scratching his head.

"Yes, and a lot more! You said something about an airship."

"Humph! Well, that's it!"

"What is?"

"An airship! I might as well tell you, I reckon. I'm having one of them contraptions made."

"What contraptions? Oh, Ezra!"

"An airship," he answered. "I'm going to have one, and win a twenty thousand dollar prize from the government. Then I'll go into the airship business and sell 'em. I'll get rich, Samantha!"

"Oh Ezra! Do you mean to say you're goin' in for any such foolishness as that?"

"'Tain't 'foolish!"

"'Tis so! And—and are you—are you goin' to go up in one of them things—them airships?"

"Well, I reckon I might. It's my machine, and I'm not going to let them aviary fellers monkey too much with it unless I'm on board. They might bust something, and want me to pay for it. Yes, I reckon I'll do some flying myself."

"Ezra Larabee!" cried his horror-stricken wife. "Be you plumb crazy?"

"I hope not, Samantha."

"But goin' up in an airship! Why it's flyin' in the face of Providence!"

"Well, it'll be flying in the air, at the same time," he chuckled. Clearly this was a different Uncle Ezra than his wife had ever known. She sighed.

"The idea!" Aunt Samantha murmured. "Goin' up in an airship. You'll fall and be killed, as sure as fate."

"That's what I was afraid of first," said Uncle Ezra, "and I didn't want to go into the scheme. But this young feller, Lieutenant Larson, he proved to me different. They can't fall. If your engine stops all you got to do is to come down like a feather. He used some funny word, but I can't think of it now. But it's safe—it's safer than farming, he claims. Most any time on a farm a bull may gore you, or a threshing engine blow up. But there's nothing like that in an airship.

"Besides, think of the twenty thousand dollars I'm going to get," he added as a final argument.

"You're not sure of it," objected his wife.

"Oh, yes I be!" he boasted. "Then I'm going into the airship business. Well, now I've told you, I'm going to sleep again."

"As if anyone could sleep after hearin' such news," she sighed. "I jest know suthin' will happen! And think what everybody will say about you! They'll say you're crazy!"

"Let 'em!" he replied, tranquilly. "They won't say so when I get that twenty thousand dollars!"

"But can't you get the money any easier way?" she wanted to know.

"How, I'd like to know? All I got to do to get this, is to get an airship to fly from New York to San Francisco."

"Why Ezra Larabee!" she exclaimed. "Now I'm sure you're not right in your head. You'll have the doctor in the mornin'."

"Oh, no, I won't!" he declared. "Don't catch me wasting any money on doctors. I'm all right."

How Aunt Samantha managed to get to sleep again she never knew. But she did, though her rest was marred by visions of airships and balloons turning upside down and spilling Mr. Larabee all over the landscape.

Mrs. Larabee renewed her objections in the morning, but her husband was firm. He had decided to have an airship built to compete for the big prize, and Larson was going to do the work.

Just what arguments the aviator had used to win over Uncle Ezra none but he himself knew. I rather think it was the harping constantly on the twenty thousand dollar prize.

That Mr. Larabee was hard to convince may easily be imagined. In fact it was learned, afterward, that the lieutenant almost gave up the attempt at one time. But he was persistent, to gain his own ends at least, and talked earnestly. Finally Uncle Ezra gave a rather grudging consent to the scheme, but he stipulated that only a certain sum be spent, and that a comparatively small one.

To this the lieutenant agreed, but I fancy with a mental reservation which meant that he would get more if he could.

At any rate preparations for building the craft, in an unused part of Uncle Ezra's woolen mill at Dankville, went on apace.

I say apace, and yet I must change that. Uncle Ezra, with his usual "closeness" regarding money, rather hampered Larson's plans.

"What do you reckon an airship ought to cost?" Mr. Larabee had asked when he first decided he would undertake it.

"Oh, I can make a good one for three thousand dollars," had been the answer of the former lieutenant.

"Three thousand dollars!" whistled Uncle Ezra. "That's a pot of money!"

"But you'll get twenty thousand dollars in return."

"That's so. Well, go ahead. I guess I can stand it." But it was not without many a sigh that the crabbed old man drew out the money from the bank, in small installments.

The work was started, but almost at once Larson demanded more than the original three thousand. Uncle Ezra "went up in the air," so to speak.

"More money!" he cried. "I shan't spend another cent!"

"But you'll have to. We want this airship to win the prize, and get ahead of the one your nephew is building. I have decided on some changes, and they will cost money."

Uncle Ezra sighed—and gave in. The truth was that Larson was little better than a sharper, and, though he did know something about aeroplanes, he knew more about how to fleece his victims.

And though Uncle Ezra furnished more money he tried to save it in other ways. He skimped on his table, until even Aunt Samantha, used as she was to "closeness," objected. Then Mr. Larabee announced a cut in wages at his factory, and nearly caused a strike.

But he was firm, and by reducing the pittance earned by the luckless operatives he managed to save a few hundred dollars which promptly went into the airship—that is, what Larson did not keep for himself.

But Uncle Ezra's airship was being built, which fact, when it became known, caused much comment. No one save Uncle Ezra and the lieutenant and his workmen, were allowed in the factory where the machine was being constructed. It was to be kept a secret as to the form of construction.

Meanwhile, having committed himself to becoming an aviator, Mr. Larabee began to study the methods of birdmen. He obtained several volumes (second hand, of course) on the history of navigating the air, and on the advance in the construction of aeroplanes. These he read diligently.

He could also have been observed going about, gazing up into the clouds, as though he was calculating from how great a height a man could fall with safety. In reality he imagined he was studying air currents.

Uncle Ezra Larabee was certainly acting most queerly, and his friends, or, rather, his acquaintances, for he had no real friends, did not know what to make of him. He did not give up his idea, however, not even when Larson raised his original estimate to five thousand dollars.

"Petrified polecats!" cried Uncle Ezra. "You'll bankrupt me, man!"

"Oh, no," answered Larson, with a winning smile. "This is getting off cheap. I want to increase the size of my mercury stabilizer to render the airship more safe for you when you go after that twenty thousand dollars."

"Well, I s'pose I've got to," sighed Uncle Ezra, and he made a careful note of how much had already been spent. "There's three thousand, nine hundred twenty-eight dollars and fourteen cents you've had so far," he reminded the lieutenant. "Don't be wasteful!"

"I won't," was the promise, easily given at least.

CHAPTER XIV

THE TRIAL FLIGHT

"All ready now; take her out!"

"Yes, and look out for the side wings! That doorway isn't any too wide."

"No. We'll have to cut some off, I guess!"

"Say, it's big; isn't it?"

These were the comments of Dick Hamilton and his chums as the fine, new airship, the Abaris, was wheeled out of the shed where it had been constructed. And certainly the young millionaire might be proud of his newest possession. Mr. Vardon and his men had labored well on the aeroplane.

It was rather a tight squeeze to get the big craft out of the barn doors, wide as they were, but it was successfully accomplished, and the craft now stood on a level stretch of grass, ready for her first trial flight.

Save for a few small details, and the stocking and provisioning of the craft in preparation for the trip across the continent, everything had been finished. The big motor had been successfully tested, and had developed even more power than had been expected. The propellers delivered a greater thrust on the air than was actually required to send the Abaris along.

"We'll have that for emergencies," said Dick. "Such as getting about in a hurricane, and the like."

"I hope we don't get into anything like that," remarked Mr. Vardon, "but if we do, I think we can weather it."

"How does the gyroscope stabilizer work?" asked Paul, who with Innis, had made Dick's house his home while the airship was being built.

"It does better than I expected," replied the inventor. "I was a bit doubtful, on account of having to make it so much larger than my first model, whether or not it would operate. But it does, perfectly,—at least it has in the preliminary tests. It remains to be seen whether or not it will do so when we're in the air, but I trust it will."

"At any rate, Larson hasn't had a chance to tamper with it," said Jack Butt, grimly.

"No, he hasn't been around," agreed Dick. "I wonder what has become of him?"

As yet the young millionaire knew nothing of the plans of his Uncle Ezra, for he had been too busy to visit his relatives in Dankville.

"Well, let's wheel her over to the starting ground," proposed Dick, as they stood around the airship. A level stretch had been prepared back of the barn, leading over a broad meadow, and above this the test flight would be made, as it offered many good landing places.

The airship was so large and heavy, as compared with the ordinary biplane, that a team of horses was used to pull it to the starting place. But heavy as it necessarily had to be, to allow the enclosed cabin to be carried, the young millionaire and his aviator hoped that the power of the motor would carry them aloft and keep them there.

"Go ahead!" cried Dick, as the team was hitched to the long rope made fast to the craft. "Take it easy now, we don't want an accident before we get started. Grit, come back here! This is nothing to get excited over," for the bulldog was wildly racing here and there, barking loudly. He did not understand the use of the big, queer-looking machine.

"Well, I'm just in time, I see!" exclaimed a voice from the direction of the house. Dick turned and cried:

"Hello, Larry, old man. I'm glad you got here. I was afraid you wouldn't," and he vigorously shook hands with the young reporter, who also greeted the other cadets. Grit leaped joyfully upon him, for he and Larry were great friends.

"Going to take her up, Dick?" asked Larry Dexter.

"Going to try," was the cautious answer.

"Want to take a chance?"

"I sure do! It won't be the first chance I've taken. And I may get a good story out of this. Got orders from the editor not to let anything get away from me."

"Well, I hope you have a success to report, and not a failure," remarked Paul.

"Same here," echoed Beeby.

When the airship had been hauled to the edge of the starting ground, a smooth, hard-packed, level space, inclining slightly down grade, so as to give every advantage, a careful inspection was made of every part of the craft.

As I have explained, all the vital parts of the Abaris were in the enclosed cabin, a unique feature of the airship. In that, located "amid-ships," was the big motor, the various controls, the living, sleeping and dining-rooms and storage compartments for oil, gasolene and supplies. Naturally there was no excess room, and quarters were almost as cramped as on a submarine, where every inch counts.

But there was room enough to move about, and have some comfort. On an enclosed platform back of the cabin there was more space. That was like an open deck, and those on it would be protected from the fierce rushing of the air, by means of the cabin. This cabin, I might add, was built wedge-shaped, with the small part pointing ahead, to cut down the air resistance as much as possible.

The big propellers were of course outside the cabin, and in the rear, where was located the horizontal rudder, for guiding the craft to right or left. At the rear was also an auxiliary vertical rudder, for elevating or lowering the craft. The main elevation rudder was in front, and this was of a new shape, never before used, as far as Mr. Vardon knew.

There was another feature of the Abaris that was new and one which added much to the comfort and safety of those aboard her. This had to do with the starting of the motor and the operation of the big wooden propellers.

In most aeroplanes, whether of the single or double type, the propeller, or propellers, are directly connected to the motor. In some monoplanes the motor, especially the Gnome, itself rotates, carrying the blades with it. In biplanes, such as the Burgess, Wright or Curtiss, it is the custom to operate the propellers directly from the motor, either by means of a shaft, or by sprocket chains.

But, in any case, the starting of the engine means the whirling of the propellers, for they are directly connected. This is why, when once the engine stops in mid-air, it can not be started again. Or at least if it is started it is mostly a matter of chance in getting it to go under compression or by the spark. There is no chance for the aviator to get out and whirl the propellers which are, in a measure, what a flywheel is to an automobile.

Also that is why the aviator has to be in his seat at the controls, and have some other person start his machine for him, by turning over the propeller, or propellers until the motor fires.

Lately however, especially since the talk of the flight across the Atlantic, a means has been found to allow the aviator, or some helper with him, to start the engine once it has stalled in midair. This is accomplished by means of a sprocket chain gear and a crank connected to the engine shaft. The turning handle is within reach of the aviator.

But Mr. Vardon, and Dick, working together, had evolved something better than this. Of course in their craft, with space to move about in the cabin, they had an advantage over the ordinary aviator, who, in case of engine trouble, has no place to step to to make an examination.

But Dick's engine was not directly connected to the propellers. There was a clutch arrangement, so that the motor could be started, with the propellers out of gear, and they could be "thrown in," just as an automobile is started. This gave greater flexibility, and also allowed for the reversing of the propellers to make a quick stop.

And it was not necessary for Dick to "crank" his motor. An electric self-starter did this for him, though in case of emergency the engine could be started by hand.

In fact everything aboard the Abaris was most up-to-date, and it was on this that Dick counted in winning the big prize.

"Well, I guess everything is as ready as it ever will be," remarked the young millionaire, as he and the aviator made a final inspection of the craft. "Get aboard, fellows!"

"He's as cheerful about it as though he were inviting us to a hanging," laughed Paul.

"Oh, I'm not worrying about any accident," said Dick quickly. "I'm only afraid we've made her too big and won't get any speed out of her. And speed is what's going to count in this trans-continental flight."

"She'll be speedy enough," predicted Mr. Vardon, with a confident air.

Paul, Innis, Larry and Mr. Vardon entered the cabin. Then Dick went in, followed by Jack Butt, who remained to tighten a guy wire that was not just to his satisfaction.

"Well, are we all here?" asked Dick, looking around.

"Yes," answered Paul, and there was a note of quiet apprehension in his voice. Indeed it was rather a risk they were all taking, but they had confidence in Mr. Vardon.

"Let her go," said Dick to the aviator.

"No, you have the honor of starting her, Mr. Hamilton," insisted Mr. Vardon, motioning to the electrical apparatus.

"All right! Here goes," announced the wealthy youth, as he pressed the starting handle. Everyone was on the alert, but nothing happened. The motor remained "dead."

"What's the trouble?" asked Dick.

"You've always got to turn that switch first, before you turn the starting handle," explained Jack.

"Oh, sure! How stupid of me!" cried Dick. "And I've started it in practice a score of times. Well, now, once more."

This time, when the switch had been thrown, the motor started at once with a throbbing roar. Faster and faster it rotated until the whole craft trembled. There was considerable noise, for the muffler was not fully closed. Dick wanted to warm-up the machinery first.

"That'll do!" shouted Mr. Vardon, who was watching the gage that told the number of revolutions per minute. "Throw in your clutch!"

"Now to see if she'll rise or not," murmured Dick. He pulled the lever that closed the muffler, thus cutting down, in a great measure, the throb of the motor. Then, with a look at his chums, he threw in the clutch. The great propellers began to revolve, and soon were flying around on their axles with the swiftness of light.

Slowly the Abaris moved forward along the ground.

"We're off!" cried Paul, excitedly.

"Not quite yet," answered Dick. "I want more power than we've got now."

He had it, almost in a moment, for the airship increased her speed across the slightly downward slope. Faster and faster she rolled along on the rubber-tired wheels.

"Now!", cried Dick, with his hand on the lever of the elevating rudder. "Look out for yourselves, fellows!"

He gave a backward pull. A thrill seemed to go through the whole craft. Her nose rose in the air. The forward wheels left the ground. Then the back ones tilted up.

Up shot the Abaris at an easy angle. Up and up! Higher and higher!

"We're doing it!" cried Dick, as he looked from the pilot house window to the earth fast falling below him. "Fellows, she's a success! We're going up toward the clouds!"

CHAPTER XV

IN DANGER

That Dick was proud and happy, and that Mr. Vardon and the chums of the young millionaire were pleased with the success of the airship, scarcely need be said. There was, for the first few moments, however such a thrill that scarcely any one of them could correctly analyze his feelings.

Of course each one of them had been in an aeroplane before. Mr. Vardon and his helper had made many flights, not all of them successful, and Dick and his fellow cadets had gone up quite often, though they were, as yet, only amateurs. Larry Dexter was perhaps less familiar with aeroplanes than any of them, but he seemed to take it as a matter of course.

"Say, this is great! Just great!" cried Dick, as he slipped the lever of the elevating rudder into a notch to hold it in place. He intended going up considerably higher.

"It sure is great, old man!" cried Paul. "I congratulate you."

"Oh, the praise belongs to Mr. Vardon," said Dick, modestly. "I couldn't have done anything without him."

"And if it hadn't been for your money, I couldn't have done anything," declared the aviator. "It all worked together."

"Say, how high are you going to take us?" asked Innis.

"Not getting scared, are you?" asked Dick, with a glance at the barograph, to ascertain the height above the earth. "We're only up about two thousand feet. I want to make it three." He looked at Mr. Vardon for confirmation.

"Three thousand won't be any too much," agreed the aviator. "She'll handle better at that distance, or higher. But until we give her a work out, it's best not to get too high."

The big propellers were whirling more and more rapidly as the motor warmed-up to its work. The craft was vibrating with the strain of the great power, but the vibration had been reduced to a minimum by means of special spring devices.

"Now we'll try a spiral ascent," said Dick, as he moved the lever of the horizontal rudder. The Abaris responded instantly, and began a spiral climb, which is usually the method employed by birdmen. They also generally descend in spirals, especially when volplaning.

Up and up went the big aircraft. There was a section of the cabin floor made of thick transparent celluloid, and through this a view could be had of the earth below.

"We're leaving your place behind, Dick," said Paul, as he noted the decreasing size of the home of the young millionaire.

"Well, we'll come back to it—I hope," Dick answered. "Don't you fellows want to try your hand at steering?"

"Wait until you've been at it a while, and see how it goes," suggested Innis. "We don't want to wreck the outfit."

But the Abaris seemed a stanch craft indeed, especially for an airship.

"Say, this is a heap-sight better than sitting strapped in a small seat, with the wind cutting in your face!" exclaimed Larry, as he moved about the enclosed cabin.

"It sure is mighty comfortable—the last word in aeroplaning, just as Dick's touring car was in autoing," declared Paul, who had taken a seat at a side window and was looking out at some low-lying clouds.

"All we want now is a meal, and we'll be all to the merry!" Dick exclaimed.

"A meal!" cried Larry. "Are you going to serve meals aboard here?"

"Yes, and cook 'em, too," answered the young millionaire. "Paul, show Larry where the galley is," for the reporter had not called at Hamilton Corners in some time, and on the last occasion the airship had been far from complete.

"Say, this is great!" Larry cried, as he saw the electrical appliances for cooking. "This is the limit! I'm glad I came along."

"We won't stop to cook now," said Mr. Vardon. "I want to see the various controls tested, to know if we have to make any changes. Now we'll try a few evolutions."

In order that all aboard might become familiar with the workings of the machinery, it was decided that there should be turn and turn about in the matter of steering and operating the craft. Reaching a height of three thousand feet, as Dick ascertained by the barograph, the young millionaire straightened his craft out on a level keel, and kept her there, sending her ahead, and in curves, at an increasing speed.

"There you go now, Paul," he called. "Suppose you take her for a while."

"Well, if you want an accident, just let me monkey with some of the works," laughed the jolly cadet. "I can do it to the queen's taste."

"You'll have to go out of your way, then," said Mr. Vardon. "I've arranged the controls so they are as nearly careless proof as possible. Just think a little bit about what you are going to do, and you won't have any trouble. It's a good thing for all of you to learn to manage the craft alone. So start in."

Paul found it easier than he expected, and he said, in spite of her bulk, that the Abaris really steered easier than one of the smaller biplanes they had gotten used to at Kentfield.

Back and forth over the fields, meadows and woods in the vicinity of Hamilton Corners the airship was taken, in charge of first one and then another of the party aboard. Larry Dexter was perhaps the one least familiar with the workings of the machine, yet even he did well, with Dick and Mr. Vardon at his side to coach him.

"Now we'll give the gyroscope stabilizer a test!" said Mr. Vardon, when each, including himself, had had a turn. "I want to make sure that it will stand any strain we can put on it."

"What are you going to do?" asked Dick.

"I'm going to tilt the craft suddenly at an angle that would turn her over if it were not for the stabilizer," was the answer.

Dick looked at the barograph, or height-recording gage. It registered thirty-eight hundred feet. They had gone up a considerable distance in making their experiments.

"Maybe you'd better wait," suggested the young millionaire, pointing to the hand of the dial, "until we go down a bit."

"No," decided the aviator. "If she's going to work at all she'll do it up at this distance as well, if not better, than she would five hundred, or one hundred feet, from the ground."

"But it might be safer—" began Paul.

"There won't be any danger—it will work, I'm sure of it," said Mr. Vardon, confidently.

The gyroscope which was depended on to keep the airship on a level keel at all times, or at least to bring her back to it if she were thrown to a dangerous angle, had been set in motion as soon as the start was made. The big lead wheel, with the bearings of antifriction metal, was spinning around swiftly and noiselessly. Once it had been started, a small impulse from a miniature electrical motor kept it going.

"Now," said Mr. Vardon, issuing his orders, "when I give the word I want you all suddenly to come from that side of the cabin to this side. At the same time, Dick, you will be at the steering wheel, and I want you to throw her head around as if you were making a quick turn for a spiral descent. That ought to throw her nearly on her beams' end, and we'll see how the gyroscope works. That will be a good test. I'll stand by to correct any fault in the gyroscope."

They were all a little apprehensive as they ranged themselves in line near one wall of the cabin. The airship tilted slightly as all the weight came on one side, just as a big excursion steamer lists to starboard or port when the crowd suddenly rushes all to one rail. But, on a steamer, deck hand are kept in readiness, with barrels of water, and these they roll to the opposite rail of the boat, thus preserving the balance.

Mr. Vardon depended on the gyroscope to perform a like service for the airship, and to do it automatically.

The aviator waited a few moments before giving the order to make the sudden rush. Already the apparatus to which was contrasted Lieutenant Larson's mercury tubes, had acted, and the Abaris, which had dipped, when all the passengers collected on one side, had now resumed her level keel again, showing that the gyroscope had worked so far at any rate.

"Now we'll give her a trial," called Mr. Vardon. "All ready, come over on the run, and throw her around, Dick!"

On the run they came, and Dick whirled the steering wheel around to the left, to cause the Abaris to swerve suddenly.

And swerve she did. With a sickening motion she turned as a vessel rolls in a heavy sea, and, at the same moment there was a dip toward the earth. The motor which had been humming at high speed went dead on the instant, and Dick Hamilton's airship plunged downward.

CHAPTER XVI

DICK IS WARNED

"What's the matter?"

"What happened?"

"We're falling!"

"Somebody do something!"

Everyone seemed talking at once, calling out in fear, and looking wildly about for some escape from what seemed about to be a fatal accident. For the Abaris was over half a mile high and was shooting toward the earth at a terrific rate.

"Wait! Quiet, everybody!" called Dick, who had not deserted his post at the steering wheel. "I'll bring her up. We'll volplane down! It'll be all right!"

His calmness made his chums feel more secure, and a glance at Mr. Vardon and his machinist aided in this. For the veteran aviator, after a quick inspection of the machinery, no longer looked worried.

"What has happened?" asked Innis.

"Our engine stalled, for some unknown reason," answered Mr. Vardon, quickly. "Fortunately nothing is broken. I'll see if I can't start it with the electrical generator. Are you holding her all right, Dick?"

"I think so; yes. I can take four or five minutes more to let her down easy."

"Well, take all the time you can. Head her up every once in a while. It will be good practice for you. The stabilizer worked all right, anyhow."

The airship was not on a level keel, but was inclined with her "bow" pointed to the earth, going downward on a slant. But Dick knew how to manage in this emergency, for many times he had practiced volplaning to earth in ordinary biplanes.

By working the lever of the vertical rudder, he now brought the head, or bow, of the airship up sharply, and for a moment the downward plunge was arrested. The Abaris shot along parallel to the plane of the earth's surface.

This operation, repeated until the ground is reached, is, as I have already explained, called volplaning.

"Something is wrong," announced Mr. Vardon, as he yanked on the lever of the starting motor, and turned the switch. Only the hum of the electrical machine resulted. The gasolene motor did not "pick up," though both the gasolene and spark levers were thrown over.

"Never mind," counseled Dick. "I can bring her down all right. There's really nothing more the matter than if we had purposely stopped the motor."

"No, that's so," agreed Mr. Vardon. "But still I want to see what the trouble is, and why it stopped. I'll try the hand starter."

But this was of no use either. The gasolene motor would not start, and without that the propellers could not be set in motion to sustain the big craft in the air. Mr. Vardon, and his helper, with the aid of Innis, Paul and Larry, worked hard at the motor, but it was as obstinate as the engine of some stalled motor-boat.

"I can't understand it," said the aviator.

"There's plenty of gasolene in the tank, and the spark is a good, fat one. But the motor simply won't start. How you making out, Dick?"

"All right. We're going to land a considerable distance from home, but maybe we can get her started when we reach the ground."

"We'll try, anyhow," agreed the aviator. "Is she responding all right?"

"Fine. Couldn't be better. Let some of the other boys take a hand at it."

"Well, maybe it would be a good plan," agreed the aviator. "You never can tell when you've got to make a glide. Take turns, boys."

"I don't think I'd better, until I learn how to run an airship that isn't in trouble," said Larry Dexter.

"Well, perhaps not," said Mr. Vardon. "But the others may."

Meanwhile the Abaris had been slowly nearing earth, and it was this slowness, caused by the gradual "sifting" down that would make it possible to land her with scarcely a jar.

If you have ever seen a kite come down when the wind has died out, you will understand exactly what this "sifting" is. It means gliding downward in a series of acute angles.

The first alarm over, all was now serene aboard Dick's airship. The attempt to start the motor had been given up, and under the supervision of Mr. Vardon the two cadets, Innis and Paul, took turns in bringing the craft down with the engine "dead." The aviator and his helper had had experience enough at this.

"Say, this is something new, guiding as big a ship as this without power," remarked Innis, as he relinquished the wheel to Paul.

"It sure is," said tile latter. Then, a little later, he called out:

"I say, somebody relieve me, quick. I believe I'm going to bring her down in that creek!"

They all looked ahead and downward. The Abaris, surely enough, was headed for a stream of water.

"Perhaps you'd better handle her," said Dick to the builder of the craft. "We don't want her wrecked before we at least have a START after that prize."

Mr. Vardon nodded, and took the wheel from Paul. A few seconds later he had brought the craft to the ground within a few feet of the edge of the stream. Had it been a wider and deeper one they could have landed on it by using the hydroplanes, but the water seemed too shallow and full of rocks for that evolution.

And so skillfully had Mr. Vardon manipulated the planes and levers that the landing was hardly felt. A number of specially-made springs took up the jar.

"Well, we're here!" exclaimed Dick, as they all breathed in relief. "Now to see what the trouble was."

"And we've got a long walk back home, in case we can't find the trouble," sighed Innis, for he was rather stout, and did not much enjoy walking. They had come down several miles from Hamilton Corners.

"Oh, we'll get her fixed up somehow," declared Dick, with confidence.

Quite a throng had gathered from the little country hamlet, on the edge of which the aircraft had descended, and they crowded up about the Abaris, looking in wonder at her size and strange shape.

Mr. Vardon lost no time in beginning his hunt for the engine trouble, and soon decided that it was in the gasolene supply, since, though the tank was nearly full, none of the fluid seemed to go into the carburetor.

"There's a stoppage somewhere," the aviator said. The fluid was drawn off into a reserve tank and then the cause of the mischief was easily located.

A small piece of cotton waste had gotten into the supply pipe, and completely stopped the flow of gasolene.

"There it is!" cried the aviator, as he took it out, holding it up for all to see.

"I wonder if anyone could have done that on purpose?" asked Dick, looking at his chums, reflectively.

"You mean—Larson?" inquired Jack Butt. "He's capable of anything like that."

"But he wasn't near the machine," said Paul.

"Not unless he sneaked in the barn some night," went on the machinist, who seemed to have little regard for the former lieutenant.

"Well, there's no way of telling for certain, so we had better say nothing about it," decided Dick. "Then, too, any of us might have accidentally dropped the waste in the tank while we were working around the ship. I guess we'll call it an accident."

"But it must have been in the tank for some time," argued Larry Dexter, "and yet it only stopped up the pipe a little while ago."

"It was probably floating around in the tank, doing no damage in particular," explained Mr. Vardon. "Then, when we made the ship tilt that way, to test the stabilizer, the gasolene shifted, and the waste was flushed into the pipe. But we're all right now."

This was proved a little later when the motor was started with no trouble whatever. There was not a very good place to make a start, along the edge of the stream, but Dick and his chums realized that they could not always have perfect conditions, so they must learn to do under adverse ones.

"Look out of the way!" warned the young millionaire to the assembled crowd. They scattered from in front of the craft. The motor throbbed and thundered up to high speed, and then the propellers were thrown into gear. The big blades beat on the air, the ship moved slowly forward. It acquired speed, and then, amid the wondering comments and excited shouts of the crowd, it soared aloft, and glided through the air to a great height.

"Off again!" cried Dick, who was at the wheel.

The trip back to Hamilton Corners was made safely, and without incident worthy of mention. The four young men took turns in working the various controls, so as to become familiar with them, and Dick paid particular attention to Larry Dexter, who needed some coaching.

"I'll get a good story out of this for my paper," said the young reporter, who was always on the lookout for "copy."

"Well, we've proved that she will fly, and take care of us even when an accident happens," remarked Dick, when the craft had been put back in the barn. "Now we'll groom her a bit, put on the finishing touches, and we'll be ready to try for that prize. The time is getting short now."

"I hope you win it," said Mr. Vardon. "I shall feel responsible, in a way, if you don't."

"Nothing of the sort!" cried Dick. "Whatever happens, I've got a fine airship, and we'll have a good time, even if we don't get the twenty thousand dollars."

The next week was a busy one, for there were several little matters about the airship that needed attention. But gradually it was made as nearly perfect as possible.

Then, one morning, Mr. Hamilton, who had some business to transact with Uncle Ezra, said to Dick:

"Could you take a run over there and leave him these securities? He asked me to get them for him out of the safe deposit box. I don't know what he wants of them, but they are his, and I have no time to take them to him myself. You can go in your airship, if you like, and give him a surprise."

"No, I think I'll go in the auto. Mr. Vardon is making a change in the motor, and it isn't in shape to run today. I'll take the boys over to Dankville in the small car."

A little later Dick and his chums were on their way to Uncle Ezra's. They reached Dankville in good time, but, on calling at the house, Aunt Samantha told them her husband was at the woolen mill.

"We'll go down there and see him," decided Dick, after talking to his aunt a little while. She had been looking in the parlor to see that, by no chance, had a glint of light gotten in. Of late her husband and his airship-partner, Larson, had not used the "best room," and so Aunt Samantha's fears about the carpet being spoiled by cigar ashes had subsided.

At the factory Dick was directed, by a foreman, to an unused wing of the building.

"You'll find your uncle in there," the man said to Dick. "He's building an airship!"

"A what!" cried the young millionaire in great astonishment, for he had been too busy, of late, to hear any news from Dankville.

"An airship—a biplane, I believe they're called," the foreman went on.

"Well, I'll be gum-swizzled!" cried Dick, faintly. "Come on, fellows. The world must be coming to an end, surely."

As he started to enter the part of the factory whither he had been directed, his uncle, plainly much excited, came out.

"Stop where you be, Nephew Richard!" he warned. "Don't come in here! Stay back!"

"Why, what in the world is the matter?" asked Dick. "Is something going to blow up?"

CHAPTER XVII

OFF FOR THE START

Uncle Ezra Larabee stood fairly glaring at his nephew. The crabbed old man seemed strangely excited.

"No, there ain't nothing going to blow up," he said, after a pause. "But don't you come in here. I warn you away! You can go in any other part of my factory you want to, but not in here."

"Well, I certainly don't want to come where I'm not wanted, Uncle Ezra," said Dick, with dignity. "But I hear you are building an airship, and I thought I'd like to get a look at it."

"And that's just what I don't want you to get—none of you," went on Mr. Larabee, looking at Dick's chums. "I don't want to be mean to my dead sister's boy," he added, "but my airship ain't in shape yet to be inspected."

"Well, if it isn't finished, perhaps we can give you some advice," said Dick, with a smile.

"Huh! I don't want no advice, thank you," said Uncle Ezra, stiffly. "I calkerlate Lieutenant Larson knows as much about building airships as you boys do."

"Larson!" cried Dick. "Is he here?"

"He certainly is, and he's working hard on my craft. I'm going to be an aviator, and win that twenty-thousand-dollar government prize!" Mr. Larabee said, as though it were a certainty.

"Whew!" whistled Dick. "Then we'll be rivals, Uncle Ezra."

"Humph! Maybe you might think so, but I'll leave you so far behind that you won't know where you are!" boasted the crabbed old man.

"Building an airship; eh?" mused Dick. "Well, that's the last thing I'd ever think of Uncle Ezra doing." Then to his relative he added: "But if you're going to compete for the prize your airship will have to be seen. Why are you so careful about it now?"

"Because we've got secrets about it," replied Mr. Larabee. "There's secret inventions on my airship that haven't been patented yet, and I don't want you going in there, Nephew Richard, and taking some of my builder's ideas and using 'em on your airship. I won't have it! That's why I won't let you in. I'm not going to have you taking our ideas, not by a jugful!"

"There's no danger," answered Dick quietly, though he wanted to laugh. "My airship is all finished. We've used her, and she's all right. I wouldn't change her no matter what I saw on yours."

"Wa'al, you might think so now, but I can't trust nobody—not even you, so you can't come in," said Uncle Ezra.

"Oh, we won't insist," answered Dick, as he passed over the bonds. "Father said you wanted these, Uncle Ezra."

"Yes, I do," and an expression, as of pain, passed over the man's face. "I've got to raise a little money to pay for this airship. It's costing a terrible pile; a terrible pile!" and he sighed in despair. "But then, of course, I'll get the twenty thousand dollars, and that will help some. After that I'm going to sell plans and models of my successful airship, and I'll make a lot more that way. So of course I'll get it all back.

"But it's costing me a terrible pile! Why, would you believe it," he said, looking around to see that the door to the factory was securely closed, "would you believe I've already spent five thousand, six hundred twenty-seven dollars and forty-nine cents on this airship? And it ain't quite done yet. It's a pile of money!"

"Yes, they are expensive, but they're worth it," said Dick. "It's great sport—flying."

"It may be. I've never tried it, but I'm going to learn," declared Uncle Ezra. "Only I didn't think it would cost so much or I never would have gone into it. But now I'm in I can't get out without losing all the money I've put up, and I can't do that. I never could do that," said Uncle Ezra with a doleful shake of his head.

He gave a sudden start, at some noise, and cried out:

"What's that? You didn't dare bring your bulldog in here, did you, Nephew Richard? If you did I'll—"

"No, I left Grit at home, Uncle Ezra."

Then the noise was repeated. It came from the part of the factory where the airship was being constructed, and was probably made by some of the workmen.

"I guess I'll have to go now," said Mr. Larabee, and this was a hint for the boys to leave.

"Lieutenant Larson said he wanted to consult with me about something. I only hope he doesn't want more money," he added with a sigh. "But he spends a terrible pile of cash—a terrible pile."

"Yes, and he'll spend a lot more of your cash before he gets through with you, if I'm any judge," thought Dick, as he and his chums went back to the automobile. "To think of Uncle Ezra building an airship! That's about the limit."

"Do you really think he is going to have a try for the government prize?" asked Larry Dexter.

"Well, stranger things have happened," admitted the young millionaire.

"You're not worrying, though, are you?" asked Paul.

"Not a bit. I imagine I'll have to compete with more formidable opponents than Uncle Ezra. But I do give Larson credit for knowing a lot about aircraft. I don't believe, though, that his mercury stabilizers are reliable. Still he may have made improvements on them. I'd like to get a look at Uncle Ezra's machine."

"And he doesn't want you to," laughed Innis. "He's a queer man, keeping track of every cent."

"Oh, it wouldn't be Uncle Ezra if he didn't do that," returned Dick, with a grin.

There were busy days ahead for the young millionaire and his chums. Though the Abaris seemed to have been in almost perfect trim on her trial trip, it developed that several changes had to be made in her. Not important ones, but small ones, on which the success, or failure, of the prize journey might depend.

Dick and his friends worked early and late to make the aircraft as nearly perfect as possible.

Dick's entry had been formally accepted by the government, and he had been told that an army officer would be assigned to make the trans-continental flight with him, to report officially on the time and performance of the craft. For the government desired to establish the nearest perfect form of aeroplane, and it reserved the right to purchase the patent of the successful model.

"And it is on that point that more money may be made than by merely winning the prize," said Mr. Vardon. "We must not forget that, so we want everything as nearly right as possible."

And to this end they worked.

"You're going to take Grit along; aren't you?" asked Paul of Dick one day, as they were laboring over the aircraft, putting on the finishing touches.

"Oh, sure!" exclaimed the young millionaire. "I wouldn't leave him behind for anything."

"I wonder what army officer they'll assign to us," remarked Innis. "I hope we get some young chap, and not a grizzled old man who'll be a killjoy."

"It's bound to be a young chap, because none of the older men have taken up aviation," said Larry. "I guess we'll be all right. I'll see if I can't find out from our Washington reporter who it will be."

But he was unable to do this, as the government authorities themselves were uncertain.

The time was drawing near when Dick was to make his start in the cross-country flight, with but two landings allowed between New York and San Francisco. Nearly everything was in readiness.

"Mr. Vardon," said Dick one day, "this business of crossing a continent in an airship is a new one on me. I've done it in my touring car, but I confess I don't see how we're going to keep on the proper course, up near the clouds, with no landmarks or anything to guide us.

"But I'm going to leave all that to you. We're in your hands as far as that goes. You'll have to guide the craft, or else tell us how to steer when it comes our turn at the wheel."

"I have been studying this matter," the aviator replied. "I have made several long flights, but never across the continent. But I have carefully charted a course for us to follow. As for landmarks, the government has arranged that.

"Along the course, in as nearly as possible a bee-line from New York to San Francisco, there will be captive balloons, painted white for day observation, and arranged with certain colored lanterns, for night-sighting. Then, too, there will be pylons, or tall towers of wood, erected where there are no balloons. So I think we can pick our course, Dick."

"Oh, I didn't know about the balloon marks," said the young millionaire. "Well, I'll leave the piloting to you. I think you know how to do it."

Several more trial flights were made. Each time the Abaris seemed to do better. She was more steady, and in severe tests she stood up well. The gyroscope stabilizer worked to perfection under the most disadvantageous conditions.

Several little changes were made to insure more comfort for the passengers on the trip. Dick's undertaking had attracted considerable attention, as had the plans of several other, and better-known aviators, to win the big prize. The papers of the country were filled with stories of the coming event, but Larry Dexter had perhaps the best accounts, as he was personally interested in Dick's success.

Dick paid another visit to Uncle Ezra, and this time his crabbed relative was more genial. He allowed his nephew to have a view of the craft Larson was building. The former lieutenant greeted Dick coldly, but our hero thought little of that. He was more interested in the machine.

Dick found that his uncle really did have a large, and apparently very serviceable biplane. Of course it was not like Dick's, as it designed to carry but three passengers.

"We're going to make the trip in about forty-eight hours, so we won't need much space," said Uncle Ezra. "We can eat a snack as we go along. And we can sleep in our seats. I've got to cut down the expense somehow. It's costing me a terrible pile of money!"

Uncle Ezra's airship worked fairly well in the preliminary trials, and though it did not develop much speed, Dick thought perhaps the crafty lieutenant was holding back on this so as to deceive his competitors.

"But, barring accidents, we ought to win," said the young millionaire to his chums. "And accidents no one can count against."

Everything was in readiness. The Abaris had been given her last trial flight. All the supplies and stores were aboard. Jack Butt had taken his departure, for he was not to make the trip. His place would be taken by the army lieutenant. A special kennel had been constructed for Grit, who seemed to take kindly to the big airship.

"Well, the officer will be here in the morning," announced Dick, one evening, on receipt of a telegram from Washington. "Then we'll make the start."

And, what was the surprise of the young millionaire and his chums, to be greeted, early the next day, by Lieutenant McBride, the officer who had, with Captain Wakefield, assisted in giving instructions at Kentfield.

"I am surely glad to see you!" cried Dick, as he shook hands with him. "There's nobody I'd like better to come along!"

"And there's nobody I'd like better to go with," said the officer, with a laugh. "I was only assigned to you at the last minute. First I was booked to go with a man named Larabee."

"He's my uncle. I'm glad you didn't!" chuckled Dick. Then he told about Larson and Lieutenant McBride, himself, was glad also.

In order to be of better service in case of an emergency, Lieutenant McBride asked that he be taken on a little preliminary flight before the official start was made, so that he might get an idea of the working of the machinery.

This was done, and he announced himself as perfectly satisfied with everything.

"You have a fine craft!" he told Dick. "The best I have ever seen, and I've ridden in a number. You ought to take the prize."

"Thanks!" laughed the young millionaire.

"Of course I'm not saying that officially," warned the officer, with a smile. "I'll have to check you up as though we didn't know one other. And I warn you that you've got to make good!"

"I wouldn't try under any other conditions," replied Dick.

The last tuning-up of the motor was over. The last of the supplies and stores were put aboard. Grit was in his place, and the cross-country fliers in theirs. Good-byes were said, and Mr. Hamilton waved the Stars and Stripes as the cabin door was closed.

"All ready?" asked Dick, who was the captain of the aircraft.

"All ready," answered Lieutenant McBride.

"All ready," agreed Mr. Vardon.

"Then here we go!" cried Dick, as he pulled the lever. The airship was on her way to the starting point.

CHAPTER XVIII

UNCLE EZRA FLIES

"Well, Mr. Larabee, we are almost ready for a flight."

"Humph! It's about time. I've sunk almost enough money in that shebang to dig a gold mine, and I haven't got any out yet—not a cent, and I'm losing interest all the while."

"Well, but think of the twenty thousand dollars!"

"Yes, I s'pose I've got to. That's the only consolation I have left."

The above conversation took place one afternoon between Ezra Larabee and Lieutenant Larson. The airship with the mercury stabilizers was nearly completed. But a few touches remained to be put on her, to make her, according to Larson, ready for the flight across the continent.

"I presume you will go with me when me make the first ascent; will you not?" the lieutenant inquired.

"Who, me? No, I don't reckon I'll go up first," said Uncle Ezra slowly. "I'll wait until I see if you don't break your neck. If you don't I'll take a chance."

"That's consoling," was the answer, with a grim laugh. "But I am not afraid. I know the craft will fly. You will not regret having commissioned me to build her."

"Wa'al, I should hope not," said Uncle Ezra, dryly. "So far I've put eight thousand, four hundred thirty-two dollars and sixteen cents into this shebang, and I ain't got a penny out yet. It just seems to chaw up money."

"They all do," said the lieutenant. "It is a costly sport. But think of the twenty-thousand-dollar prize!"

"I do," said Uncle Ezra, softly. "That's all that keeps me from thinking what a plumb idiot I've been—thinking of that twenty thousand dollars."

"Oh, you'll get it!" the lieutenant asserted.

"Maybe—yes. If my nephew doesn't get ahead of me," was the grim reply.

"Oh, he never will. We'll win that prize," the lieutenant assured him. "Now there's one other little matter I must speak of. I need some more money."

"More money! Good land, man! I gave you three dollars and a half last week to buy something!" cried Uncle Ezra.

"Yes, I know, but that went for guy wires and bolts. I need about ten dollars for an auxiliary steering wheel."

"A steering wheel?" questioned Uncle Ezra. "You mean a wheel to twist?"

"That's it. There must be two. We have only one."

"Well, if it's only a wheel, I can fix you up about that all right, and without spending a cent, either!" exclaimed the stingy old man with a chuckle. "There's an old sewing machine of my wife's down cellar. It's busted, all but the big wheel. We had an accident with it, but I made the company give me a new machine, and I kept the old one.

"Now that's got a big, round, iron wheel on it, and we can take that off, just as well as not, and use it on the airship. That's what you've got to do in this world—save money. I've spent a terrible pile, but we'll save some by using the sewing machine wheel."

"It won't do," said the lieutenant. "It's far too heavy. I must have one made to order of wood. It will cost ten dollars."

"Oh, dear!" groaned Uncle Ezra. "More money," and he looked distressed. Then his face brightened.

"I say!" he cried. "There's a busted mowing machine out in the barn. That's got a wooden wheel on it. Can't you use that?"

Lieutenant Larson shook his head.

"It's no use trying to use make-shift wheels if we are to have a perfect machine, and win the prize," he said. "I must have the proper one. I need ten dollars."

"Oh, dear!" moaned Uncle Ezra, as he took out his wallet, and carefully counted out ten one-dollar bills.

"Couldn't you look around and get a second-hand one?" he asked hopefully.

"No; we haven't time. We must soon start on the prize trip. We don't want to be late."

"No, I s'pose not. Wa'al, take the money," and he parted with it, after a long look. Then he made a memoranda of it in his pocket cash-book, and sighed again.

Several times after this Lieutenant Larson had to have more money—or, at least, he said he needed it, and Uncle Ezra brought it forth with many sighs and groans. But he "gave up."

To give Larson credit, he had really produced a good aircraft. Of course it was nothing like Dick's, and, after all, the former army man was more interested in his stabilizers than he was in the airship itself. But he had to build it right and properly to give his patent a good test, and he used his best ideas on the subject.

In general Uncle Ezra's machine was a biplane, a little larger than usual, and with a sort of auxiliary cabin and platform where one could rest when not in the seats. Three passengers could be carried, together with some food and supplies of gasolene and oil. It was an airship built for quick, continuous flight, and it really had a chance for the prize; perhaps not as good a chance as had Dick's, but a good chance compared with others in its class. The one weak point, and this Lieutenant Larson kept to himself, was the fact that it was only with the best of luck that the flight could be made with but two landings.

Finally the former army man announced that the craft was ready for a flight. He had spent all the money Uncle Ezra would give him—nearly ten thousand dollars—and I suspect that Larson himself had lined his own pockets well.

"She's ready," he announced to Uncle Ezra, one day.

"Well, take her up."

"Will you come?"

"Not till I see how you fare. Go ahead."

"Ezra, be you goin' up in that contraption?" asked Aunt Samantha, as she came out in the meadow where a starting ground had been laid out.

"I'm aiming to, if he comes back alive with it," Uncle Ezra made answer, grimly.

"Well, as I said before, it's flyin' in the face of Providence," declared Mrs. Larabee. "I might as well order my mourning now, and be done with it."

"Oh, I ain't aiming to be killed," chuckled Uncle Ezra. "I guess it's safe enough. I've got to get my money back out of this thing."

Lieutenant Larson, with one of the helpers, made the first flight. He did not go very high, so that Uncle Ezra would have confidence. When he came back to the starting point he asked:

"Well, will you take a chance?"

"I—I guess so," replied Mr. Larabee, and his voice was not very steady.

"I'm goin' in the house," announced Mrs. Larabee. "I don't want to see it!"

Uncle Ezra took his place.

"I've got accident insurance in case anything happens," he said, slowly.

"I don't believe your policy covers airship flights," the lieutenant returned.

"Then let me out!" cried Uncle Ezra. "I'll have the policy changed! I'm not going to take any such chances!"

"It's too late!" cried Larson. "Here we go!" The engine was thundering away, and a moment later the craft shot over the ground and into the air. Uncle Ezra was flying at last.

CHAPTER XIX

UNCLE EZRA'S ACCIDENT

For some seconds after he had been taken up in the atmosphere in his airship, Uncle Ezra said nothing. He just sat there in the padded seat, clutching with his hands the rails in so tight a grip that his knuckles showed white.

Up and up they went, Larson skillfully guiding the craft, until they were a considerable distance above the earth.

"That's—that's far enough!" Uncle Ezra managed to yell, above the throb of the now throttled-down motor. "Don't go—any higher!"

"All right," agreed the aviator. "But she'll work easier up a little more."

"No—it—it's too far—to fall!" said Mr. Larabee, and he could not keep his voice from trembling.

Really, though, he stood it bravely, though probably the thought of all the money he had invested in the craft, as well as the prize he was after, buoyed up his spirits.

"How do you like it?" asked Larson, when they had circled around over Mr. Larabee's extensive farm for some time.

"It's different from what I expected," remarked Uncle Ezra. "But it seems good. I don't know as I'll stand it all the way to San Francisco, though."

"Oh, yes, you will," asserted Larson. "You'll get used to it in time."

"Is she working all right, Lieutenant Larson?"

"Yes, pretty well. I see a chance to make one or two changes though, that will make her better."

"Does that mean—er—more money?" was Uncle Ezra's anxious question.

"Well, some, yes."

"Not another cent!" burst out the crabbed old man. "I won't spend another cent on her. I've sunk enough money in the old shebang."

Larson did not answer. He simply tilted the elevating rudder and the biplane poked her nose higher up into the air.

"Here! What you doing?" demanded Uncle Ezra.

"I'm going up higher."

"But I tell you I don't want to! I want to go down! This is high enough!" and Uncle Ezra fairly screamed.

"We've got to go higher," said Larson. "The carburetor isn't working just right at this low elevation. That's what I wanted the extra money for, to get a new one. But of course if you feel that you can't spare it, why, we'll simply have to fly higher, that's all. The carburetor we have will work all right at a high elevation on account of the rarefied air, but with a different one, of course we could stay lower—if we wanted to.

"Still, if you feel you can't afford it," he went on, with a sly look at the crabbed old man who sat there clutching the sides of the seat, "we'll have to do the best we can, and make this carburetor do. I guess we'll have to keep on a little higher," he added, as he glanced at the barograph.

"Say! Hold on!" yelled Uncle Ezra in his ear. "You—you can have that money for the carburetor! Go on down where we were before."

"Oh, all right," assented Larson, and he winked the eye concealed from his employer.

The aircraft went down, and flew about at a comparatively low elevation. Really, there did not seem to be much the matter with the carburetor, but then, of course, Larson ought to know what he was talking about.

"She's working pretty good—all except the carburetor," said the former army man, after they had been flying about fifteen minutes. "The motor does better than I expected, and with another passenger we'll be steadier. She needs a little more weight. Do you want to try to steer her?"

"No, sir! Not yet!" cried Uncle Ezra. "I can drive a mowing-machine, and a thresher, but I'm not going to try an airship yet. I hired you to run her. All I want is that twenty-thousand-dollar prize, and the chance to sell airships like this after we've proved them the best for actual use."

"And we can easily do that," declared Larson. "My mercury stabilizer is working to perfection."

"When can we start on the race?" Mr. Larabee wanted to know.

"Oh, soon now. You see it isn't exactly a race. That is the competing airships do not have to start at the same time."

"No?" questioned Uncle Ezra.

"No. You see each competing craft is allowed to start when the pilot pleases, provided an army officer is aboard during the entire flight to check the results, and the time consumed. Two landings will be allowed, and only the actual flying time will be counted.

"That is if the trip is finished within a certain prescribed time. I think it is a month. In other words we could start now, fly as far as we could, and if we had to come down because of some accident, or to get supplies, we could stay down several days. Then we could start again, and come down the second time. But after that we would be allowed no more landings, and the total time consumed in flying would be computed by the army officer."

"Oh, that's the way of it?" asked Uncle Ezra.

"Yes, and the craft that has used the smallest number of hours will win the prize," went on Larson. "I'm sure we can do it, for this is a fast machine. I haven't pushed her to the limit yet."

"And don't you do it—not until I get more used to it," stipulated the owner of the airship.

The former army officer sent the aircraft through several simple evolutions to test her. She answered well, though Uncle Ezra gasped once or twice, and his grip on the seat rail tightened.

"When do you plan to start?" Mr. Larabee wanted to know, again.

"Oh, in about a week. I have sent in an application to have a representative of the government assigned to us, and when he comes we'll start. That will give me a chance to buy the new carburetor, and make some other little changes."

"Well, let's go down now," suggested Uncle Ezra. "Hello, what's this?" he cried, looking at his coat. "Why, I'm all covered with oil!"

"Yes, it does drip a little," admitted the aviator. "I haven't tightened the washers on the tank. You mustn't mind a little thing like that. I often get soaked with oil and gasolene. I should have told you to put on an old suit."

"But look here!" cried Uncle Ezra, in accents of dismay. "I didn't put on an old suit! This is my second best. I paid thirteen dollars for it, and I've bad it four years. It would have been good for two more if your old oil hadn't leaked on it. Now it's spoiled!"

"You can have it cleaned, perhaps," suggested the lieutenant as he sent the biplane about in a graceful curve, before getting ready for a descent.

"Yes, and maybe have to pay a tailor sixty-five cents! Not much!" cried Uncle Ezra. "I'll clean it myself, with some of the gasolene. I ain't going to waste money that way. I ought to charge you for it."

"Well, I'll give you the gasolene to clean it," said the aviator, with another unseen wink.

"Humph!" ejaculated Uncle Ezra with a grunt, as he tried to hold on with one hand, and scrub off some of the oil spots with his handkerchief.

"Well, I guess we'll go down now," announced Larson, after making several sharp ascents and descents to test the efficiency of the vertical rudder.

"Why, we're quite a way from the farm!" exclaimed Mr. Larabee, looking down. "I didn't think we'd come so far."

"Well, I'll show you how quickly we can get back there!" boasted Larson. "I'll have you at your place in a hurry!"

He turned more power into the motor, and with a rush and a roar, the biplane shot forward.

But something happened. Either they struck an air pocket, or the rudder was given too sudden a twist. Anyway, the airship shot toward the ground at a sharp angle. She would have crashed down hard, only Larson threw her head up quickly, checking, in a measure, the momentum.

But he could not altogether control the craft, and it swept past a tree in an orchard where they were forced to land, the side wing tearing off the limbs and branches.

Then, bouncing down to the ground, the airship, tilted on one end, and shot Uncle Ezra out with considerable force. He landed in a heap of dirt, turned a somersault, and sat up with a queer look on his face.

CHAPTER XX

IN NEW YORK.

"Well, this is going some!"

"I should say yes!"

"All to the merry!"

"And no more trouble than as if you got in a taxicab and told the chauffeur to take you around the block."

Thus did Dick Hamilton's chums offer him their congratulations as they started off on the trip they hoped would bring to the young millionaire the twenty-thousand-dollar prize, and, not only do that but establish a new record in airship flights, and also give to the world the benefit of the experience in building such a unique craft.

They were in the Abaris flying along over the town of Hamilton Corners, a most successful start having been made. As they progressed through the air many curious eyes were turned up to watch their flight.

"I say! Which way are you steering?" asked Paul, as he came back from a trip to the dining-room buffet, where he had helped himself to a sandwich, a little lunch having been set out by Innis, who constituted himself as cook. "You're heading East instead of West, Dick," for the young millionaire was at the steering-wheel.

"I know it," replied the helmsman, as he noted the figures on the barograph. "But you see, to stand a chance for the prize you've got to start from New York, and that's where we're headed for now. We've got to go to the big town first, and then we'll hit the Western trail as nearly in a straight line as we can."

"That's the idea," said Lieutenant McBride. "The conditions call for a start from New York, and I have arranged for the beginning of your flight from the grounds at Fort Wadsworth. That will give the army officers there a chance to inspect your machine, Mr. Hamilton."

"And I'll be very glad to have them see it," Dick said, "and to offer their congratulations to Mr. Vardon on his success."

"And yours, too," added the aviator. "I couldn't have done anything had it not been for you."

"Then we really aren't on the prize winning flight, yet?" asked Larry, who wanted to get all the information he could for his paper.

"Not exactly," replied the lieutenant. "And yet the performance of the airship will count on this flight, in a measure. I have been instructed to watch how she behaves, and incorporate it in my report. It may be, Mr. Hamilton, though I hope not, that the prize will not come to you. But you may stand a chance of having your airship adopted by Uncle Sam, for all that."

"That would be a fine feather in my cap!" cried Dick. "I don't care so much for the money, I guess you all know that."

"I should say not!" cried Innis, with a laugh.

"Any fellow who's worth a million doesn't have to bother about a little small change like twenty thousand dollars."

"Not that I haven't a due regard for the prize," went on Dick. "But if I lost it, and still could have the honor of producing an airship that would be thought worthy of government approval, that would be worth while."

"Indeed it would!" agreed the lieutenant.

"Are we going to have any time at all in New York?" asked Paul. "I have some friends there, and—"

"I believe her name is Knox; isn't it?" interrupted Innis, with a grin at his chum. "First name Grace, lives somewhere up in Central Park, West, eh, old chap?"

"Oh, dry up!" invited Paul. "Don't you s'pose I've got any friends but girls?"

"Well, Grace does live in New York," insisted Innis.

"Yes, and so do Irene Martin and Mabel Hanford!" burst out Paul. "It's as much on you fellows as it is on me," and he fairly glared at his tormentor.

"Easy!" laughed Dick. "I guess we may as well make a family party of it while we're about it. Of course we'll see the girls. In fact I half-promised Miss Hanford I'd call on her if I could get my airship to work."

"Oh, you sly dog!" mocked Innis. "And you never said a word!"

"I didn't know I could get it to work," laughed Dick, as he stood at the wheel.

The Abaris was cleaving through the clear air at a fast rate of speed, though she was not being sent along at her limit. The aviator wanted to test his machinery at moderate speed for some time before he turned on full power, and this trip to New York for the start gave him the very chance wanted.

It was a journey of about five hundred miles from Hamilton Corners to New York City, and, as Dick and his friends had planned it, they would be in the air all night.

They had set for themselves a rate of progress of about fifty miles an hour, and if this was kept up it would take ten hours to the metropolis.

Of course the journey could have been made in much less time than that, for Dick's motor was calculated to give a maximum speed of one hundred miles an hour. But this was straining it to its capacity. It would be much more feasible, at, least on this trial trip, to use half that speed. Later, if need be, they could go to the limit.

They had started late in the afternoon, and by journeying at fifty miles an hour they would reach the upper part of New York city in the morning; that is if nothing occurred to delay them. But the weather predictions were favorable, and no storms were in prospect.

"I think I'll take her up a bit," remarked Dick, when they had passed out over the open country, lying outside of Hamilton Corners. "We might as well get used to good heights, for when we cross the Rocky Mountains we'll have to ascend some."

"That's right," agreed the lieutenant. "Take her up, Dick."

The young millionaire pulled over the lever of the vertical rudder, and as the nose of the Abaris was inclined upward, she shot aloft, her big propellers in the rear pushing her ahead.

"I'm going out on the outer deck and see how it seems," said Larry. "I want to get some new impressions for the paper. I told the editor we'd pull off a lot of new stunts. So I guess I'll go outside."

"No, you won't," said Lieutenant McBride, laying a detaining hand on the arm of the reporter. "Do you see that notice?"

He pointed to one over the door. It read:

"No one will be allowed on the outer deck while the airship is ascending or descending."

"What's that for?" Larry wanted to know.

"So you won't roll off into space," replied Lieutenant McBride. "You see the deck is much tilted, when we are going up or down, and that makes it dangerous. Of course the cabin floor is tilted also, but there are walls here to save you from taking a tumble in case you slip. Outside there is only a railing."

"I see," spoke Larry. "Well, I'll stay inside until we get up as high as Dick wants to take us."

"Not very high this time," the young millionaire answered. "About six thousand feet will be enough. We haven't gone quite a mile yet, and it will be a good test for us."

Steadily the aircraft climbed upward until, when he had noted from the barograph that they were at a height of nearly six thousand feet, Dick "straightened her out," and let her glide along on a level keel.

"You may now go outside, Larry," said the lieutenant, and the young reporter and the others, except Dick, who remained at the wheel, took their places in the open.

It was a strange sensation standing out thus, on a comparatively frail craft, shooting along at fifty miles an hour over a mile above the earth. The cabin broke the force of the wind, and there was really little discomfort. The Abaris sailed so steadily that there was scarcely a perceptible motion. Larry made some notes for a story on which he was engaged. He wrote it in his best style, and then enclosed the "copy" in a leather case.

"I'm going to drop this when we are passing over some city," he explained. "Someone is sure to pick it up, and I've put a note in saying that if they will file the copy at some telegraph office, so it can be sent to my paper, they'll get five dollars on presentation of my note."

"Good idea!" cried Dick.

"Oh, I've got to get the news to the office, somehow," said Larry with a smile.

A little later they passed over a large town, and, though they did not know the name of it, Larry dropped his story and eventually, as he learned later, it reached the office safely, and made a hit.

In order that all might become familiar with the workings of the airship, Dick, after a while, relinquished the wheel to one of his chums. Thus they took turns guiding the craft through the air, and gained valuable experience.

They flew along easily, and without incident, until dusk began to overcast the sky, and then the electric lamps were set aglow, and in the cosy cabin they gathered about the table on which Innis had spread a tempting lunch.

"Say, this sure is going some!" cried Larry, as he took another helping of chicken, prepared on the electric stove. "Think of dining a mile in the air!"

"As long as we don't fall down while we're dining, I shan't mind," mumbled Paul, as he picked a wishbone.

The night passed without incident of moment. For a time no one wanted to go to the comfortable bunks, but Dick insisted that they must get used to sleeping aboard his craft, so the watch was told off, two of the occupants of the Abaris to be on duty for two hours at a time, to be relieved by others.

On and on rushed the airship. Now and then she was speeded up for a time, as Dick and the aviator wanted to see what she could do when called on suddenly. She responded each time.

"I think she'll do," said Lieutenant McBride, when it came his turn to take a little rest. "You have a fine craft, Mr. Hamilton."

"Glad of it," responded Dick. "We'll see what she does when we straighten her out on the long run to San Francisco."

The night wore on. Above the earth, like some gigantic meteor, flew the airship, her propellers forcing her onward and onward. Now and then some of the machinery needed attention, but very little. The gyroscope stabilizer worked well, and as it was automatic, there was no need of warping the wing tips, or of using the alerons, which were provided in case of emergency. The Abaris automatically kept herself on a level keel, even as a bird does when flying.

The gray dawn crept in through the celluloid windows of the aircraft. This material had been used instead of glass, to avoid accidents in case of a crash. The celluloid would merely bend, and injure no one.

"It's morning!" cried Dick, as he sprang from his bunk, for he had had the previous watch.

"Morning?" repeated Innis. "Well, where are we?"

"Have to go down and take an observation," suggested the lieutenant. "I think we must be very near New York."

Paul, who was in charge of the wheel looked for confirmation to Dick. The latter nodded, and the cadet pulled the lever that would send the airship on a downward slant.

It was not long before a group of big buildings came into view. It needed but a glance to tell what they were sky-scrapers.

"New York!" cried Dick. "We're over New York all right!"

"Then I've got to get a message to my paper!" exclaimed Larry. "Is the wireless working?"

"We'll have to make a landing to send it up," replied Mr. Vardon.

"Well, if we're going down anyhow, a telephone will do as well," went on the reporter. "Only it's going to be a job to land down among all those sky scrapers."

"We can't do it," Mr. Vardon declared.

"We'll have to head for an open space."

"Central Park, or the Bronx," put in the lieutenant. "Either place will give us room enough."

"We'll try the Bronx," suggested Dick. "That will give us a chance to see New York from aloft. We'll land in the Bronx."

They had sailed over to the metropolis from a point about opposite Jersey City, and now they took a direct Northward course flying lengthwise over Manhattan.

As they came on down and down, they were observed by thousands of early workers, who craned their necks upward, and looked with eager eyes at the big airship over their heads.

A few minutes of flying over the city brought the aviators within sight of the big beautiful Zoological Park which is the pride of New York. Below Dick and his chums stretched out the green expanses, the gardens, the little lakes, and the animal enclosures.

"There's a good place!" exclaimed Dick, pointing to a green expanse near the wild-fowl pond.

"Then you take the wheel and make it," suggested Innis, who had been steering.

Dick did so, but his hand accidentally touched the gasolene lever, cutting off the supply to the motor. In an instant the machine went dead.

"Never mind!" cried the young millionaire. "I'll go down anyhow. No use starting the motor again. I'll volplane and land where I can."

And, as it happened, he came down in New York, in the midst of the Bronx Park buffalo range.

It was a perfect landing, the Abaris reaching the ground with scarcely a jar. But the big, shaggy buffaloes snorted in terror, and ran in all directions. That is, all but one big bull, and he, with a bellow of rage, charged straight for the airship!

CHAPTER XXI

OFF FOR THE PACIFIC

"Look out for him!"

"Go up in the air again!"

"Has anybody got a gun?"

"Start the motor!"

These, and other excited cries, came from those in Dick Hamilton's airship as they saw the charging buffalo. The animal was the largest in the captive herd, probably the leader. It seemed a strange thing for a modern airship to be threatened with an attack by a buffalo in these days, but such was the case.

"He may damage us!" cried Dick. "We've got to do something!"

But there seemed nothing to do. Before they could get out of the cabin of the airship, which now rested on the ground within the buffalo range, the frightened and infuriated animal might rush at the craft.

And, though he would probably come off second best in the odd battle, he might damage some of the frail planes or rudders.

"Come on!" cried Paul. "Let's all rush out at him at once, and yell as hard as we can. That may scare him off."

But there was no need of this. Before the buffalo had time to reach the airship a mounted police officer rode rapidly up to the fence of the enclosure, and, taking in the situation, novel as it was, at a glance, he fired several shots from his revolver at the rushing animal.

None of the bullets was intended to hit the buffalo, and none did. But some came so close, and the noise of the shots was so loud, that the beast stopped suddenly, and then, after a pause, in which he snorted, and pawed the ground, he retreated, to stand in front of the herd of cows and other bulls, probably thinking he constituted himself their protector against the strange and terrible foe.

"Well, that's over!" exclaimed Dick, with a sigh of relief. "Say, isn't this the limit? If we bad an airship out on the plains fifty years ago it wouldn't have been any surprise to be charged by a buffalo. But here in New York—well, it is just about the extreme edge, to my way of thinking!"

"All's well that ends well," quoted Innis. "Now let's get breakfast."

But it seemed that something else was to come first.

"Get your craft out of there," ordered the police officer, who had fired the shots.

"I guess we'd better," said Dick to his chums. "That buffalo might change his mind, and come at us again."

"How are we going to get out?" asked Mr. Vardon, as he noticed the heavy fence around the buffalo enclosure. And there was hardly room inside it to get the necessary start to raise the big airship.

"I'll unlock this gate for you, and you can wheel her out," said the officer, who seemed to know something about aircraft. He rode over to a double gate, which he soon swung open, and Dick and his chums, by considerable exertion, managed to wheel the airship out on the walk. The slope of the buffalo enclosure was downward or they might not have been successful.

"Now then," went on the mounted policeman, when he had locked the gate to prevent any of the animals from straying out, "who's in charge of this outfit?"

"I am," admitted Dick, as his chums looked at him.

"Well then, I'm sorry, but I have to place you under arrest," spoke the officer. "You'll have to come with me."

"Arrest! What for?" gasped Dick.

"Two charges. Entering the buffalo enclosure without a permit, and flying an airship over a city. I saw you come from down New York way."

For a moment those of Dick's aviation party hardly knew whether to treat the matter as a joke or not, but a look at the face of the officer soon convinced them that he, at least, was in earnest.

"Under arrest!" murmured Dick. "Well, I guess the two charges are true, as far as that goes. We did fly over the city, but there was no harm in that, and—"

"Hold on—yes, there was!" exclaimed Mr. Vardon. "It was stupid of me to forget it, too. It is against the law now for an aeroplane to fly over a city, and contrary to the agreement of the association of aviators."

"You are right!" exclaimed Lieutenant McBride. "I should have thought of that, too, but I was so interested watching the working of the machinery I forgot all about it. The rule and the law was made because of the danger to persons over whose heads the aeroplanes might fly—that is, not so much danger in the flying as in the coming down. And then, too, as a general thing it might not be safe for the aviators if they were forced to make a landing. But we've gone and done it, I guess," and he smiled frankly at the officer.

"As for coming down in the buffalo enclosure, I was sorry we did it when I saw that old bull coming for us," remarked Dick. "But it seemed the best place around here for us to land, after our motor stopped. I suppose it won't do any good to say we're sorry; will it?" he asked the policeman, with a smile.

"Well, I shall have to do my duty, and arrest you," said the officer, "but I will explain to the magistrate that you did not mean to land contrary to the law."

"Who is the magistrate before whom we shall have to appear?" asked Larry Dexter.

"Judge Scatterwaite," was the answer.

"Good!" cried the young reporter. "I know him. My paper supported him in the last campaign, and I believe he will be glad to do a favor for me. Is there a telephone around here?" he asked the officer. "Oh, we won't run away," he hastened to assure the guardian of the peace. "I just want to talk to the judge. I'm Larry Dexter, of the Leader."

"Oh, is that so? I guess I've heard of you. Aren't you the reporter who worked up that stolen boy case?"

"I am," admitted Larry, modestly. "There's a telephone right over there, in the Rocking Stone restaurant," went on the officer, who seemed to regard Larry and his friends in a different light now. "You can call up the judge. He'll probably be at his house now. I'll go with you. It may be that he will want to speak to me, and will dismiss the complaint."

"We'll wait here for you, Larry," said Dick. "There's nothing like having a reporter with you when you break the law," he added, with a laugh.

The officer rode his horse slowly along with Larry, going to the place whence a telephone message could be sent. Larry was soon talking with the judge, who, on learning the identity of the young reporter, and having heard the circumstances, spoke to the officer.

"It's all right!" exclaimed the policeman, as he hung up the receiver. "I'm to let you go. He says he'll find you all guilty, and will suspend sentence."

"Good!" cried Larry. "That's the time my 'pull' was of some use."

"And I'm glad I didn't have to take you to the station," the mounted man proceeded. "I'm interested in airships myself. I've got a boy who's crazy about them, and wireless. He's got a wireless outfit—made it all himself," he added, proudly.

There was nothing further to worry the aviators, on the return of Larry with the officer, so they prepared to have breakfast, and then Lieutenant McBride said he would arrange to have the official start in the prize race made from Fort Wadsworth.

"But we'll have to fly over New York again," suggested Dick, "and if we're arrested a second time—"

"I think I can arrange that for you," said the army man. "I will have the war department make a request of the civil authorities who will, no doubt, grant permission to soar over the city."

"Good!" cried Dick. "And now for breakfast. Didn't that officer say something about a restaurant around here?"

"Yes, I telephoned from one," spoke Larry. "Then let's go there and have breakfast," suggested the young millionaire. "We'll have a little more room than in the airship, and Innis won't have to do the cooking."

"Oh, I don't mind," the stout cadet put in.

"What about leaving the airship all alone?" asked Paul, for already a crowd had gathered about it.

"I'll look out for it while you're gone," promised the officer.

"Isn't there some shed around here where we could leave it, so it would be safe?" asked Innis.

"What's the idea of that?" Dick wanted to know. "We'll be sailing down to the fort in an hour or so."

"Why can't we stay over a day or so in New York?" went on Innis. "I don't get here very often, and I'd like to see the sights."

"You mean you'd like to see the girls!" declared Paul, laughingly.

"Have your own way," murmured Innis. "But, if the airship would be safe up here in the park, in a shed, we could take our time, and not have to hurry so."

"I guess that would be a good plan," agreed Dick. "I'd like to see the girls myself. We'll do it if we can find a shed."

The obliging officer arranged this for them, and the airship was soon safely housed, a watchman being engaged to keep away the curious. Then our friends went to breakfast, and, later, down town.

Mr. Vardon wanted to call on some fellow aviators, now that it had been decided to postpone the start a day, and Larry Dexter had some business to transact at the newspaper office.

"And we'll go see the girls!" cried Dick.

Mabel Hanford, Grace Knox and Irene Martin, the three young ladies in whom the boys were more than ordinarily interested, had come on to New York, after their school closed, and our friends had made a half-promise to meet them in the metropolis. Now the promise could be kept. They found the girls at a hotel, where they resided part of the year, and, sending up their cards, were ushered to their sitting-room.

"And did you really come all the way from Hamilton Corners to New York in your airship?" asked Mabel of Dick.

"We surely did," he answered. "And we're going to start for San Francisco tomorrow. We just stopped overnight to see you."

"We appreciate the honor," laughed Irene, with a bow.

"Have you any engagement for tonight?" asked Innis.

"We were going to the theatre," said Grace.

"Isn't there any place we could go to a dance?" inquired Paul.

"Say, he's crazy on these new dances!" exclaimed Dick. "I caught him doing the 'lame duck' the other night, with the broom for a partner."

"Oh, do you do that?" cried Mabel.

"A little," admitted Paul.

"Will you show us how the steps go?" asked Irene.

"And I know the 'lace glide,' and the 'pivot whirl,'" put in Dick. "You needn't think you can walk off with all the honors," he said to his chum, laughingly.

"Oh, let's stay at the hotel and dance tonight," suggested Mabel. "Mamma will chaperone us. It will be more fun than the theatre."

"We'll have to hire dress suits," said Innis. "We didn't bring them in the airship."

"No, we'll make it very informal," Grace remarked. "There is a little private ballroom we can engage."

So it was arranged, and the young people spent an enjoyable evening, doing some of the newest steps.

"We'll come down to the fort in the morning, and see you start for San Francisco," promised Mabel, as she said good-night to Dick.

"Will you!" he exclaimed. "That will be fine of you!"

An early morning start was made for the fort, after the airship, which had been left in Bronx Park all night, had been carefully gone over. An additional supply of gasolene was taken aboard, some adjustments made to the machinery, and more food put in the lockers.

"There are the girls!" exclaimed Dick, after they had made a successful landing at the fort, which they would soon leave on their long flight.

"Oh, so they are! I hardly thought they'd come down," observed Paul, as he waved to the three pretty girls with whom they had danced the night before.

"I wish we were going with you!" cried Mabel, as she greeted Dick.

"Oh, Mabel! You do not!" rebuked Irene.

"Well, I just do!" was the retort. "It's so stupid just staying at a summer resort during the hot weather."

"We'll come back, after we win the prize, and do the 'aeroplane glide' with you," promised Innis.

"Will you?" demanded Irene. "Remember now, that's a promise."

Final arrangements were made, and everything was in readiness for the start for the Pacific. The army officers had inspected the craft, and congratulated the young owner and the builder on her completeness.

"Well, good-bye, girls," said Dick, as he and his chums shook hands with their friends who had come to see them off. The aviators took their places in the cabin. A hasty inspection showed that everything was in readiness.

"Well, here we go!" murmured Dick.

He turned the switch of the electric starter, and, an instant later, the Abaris shot forward over the ground, rising gracefully on a long, upward slant.

Then Dick, who was at the steering wheel, headed his craft due West.

From the parade ground below them came cheers from the army men and other spectators, the shrill cries of the three girls mingling.

"I wonder what will happen before we dance with them again?" spoke Paul, musingly.

"You can't tell," answered Innis, as he looked down for a last sight of a certain pretty face.

"Well, we can only hit the ground twice between here and San Francisco," remarked Dick, as he turned on more power. "If we have to come down the third time—we lose the prize."

"We're not going to lose it!" asserted Mr. Vardon, earnestly.

Of course there were many more entrants for the prize than Dick Hamilton. Two airships had started that morning before he got off in his craft, and three others were to leave that afternoon. One prominent birdman from the West was due to start the next day, and on the following two from the South were scheduled to leave. There were also several well-known foreigners who were making a try for the fame, honor and money involved.

But this story only concerns Dick Hamilton's airship, and the attempt of himself, and his Uncle Ezra, to win the prize, and I have space for no more than a mere mention of the other contestants.

CHAPTER XXII

UNCLE EZRA STARTS OFF

Let us now, for a moment, return to Uncle Ezra. We left him sitting on the ground after his rather unceremonious exit from the airship which had crashed into the apple tree in the orchard. Somehow the strap, holding him to his seat, had come unbuckled, which accounted for his plight.

"Are you hurt?" asked Lieutenant Larson, after a quick glance that assured him the airship was not badly damaged.

"I don't know's I'm hurt such a terrible lot," was the slow answer, "but my clothes are all dirt. This suit is plumb ruined now. I swan I'd never have gone in for airships if I knew how expensive they'd be. This suit cost thirteen dollars and—"

"You're lucky you don't have to pay for a funeral," was the lieutenant's grim answer. "You must look to your seat strap better than that."

"Well, I didn't know the blamed thing was going to cut up like this!" returned the crabbed old man. "That's no way to land."

"I know it. But I couldn't help it," was the answer. "I'm glad you're not hurt. But I think we have attracted some attention. Here comes someone."

A man was running through the orchard.

"It's Hank Crittenden, and he hates me like poison!" murmured Uncle Ezra, as he arose from the pile of dirt, and tried to get some of it off his clothes.

"Hi, there! What's this mean?" demanded Hank, as he rushed up, clutching a stout club. "What d'ye mean, comin' down in my orchard, and bustin' up my best Baldwin tree? What d'ye mean?"

"It was an accident—purely an accident," said Lieutenant Larson, suavely. "It could not be helped."

"Accident? You done it on puppose, that's what you did!" cried Hank, glaring at Uncle Ezra. "You done it on puppose, and I'll sue ye for damages, that's what I'll do! That Baldwin apple tree was one of the best in my orchard."

"Well, we didn't mean to do it," declared Mr. Larabee. "And if you sue we can prove in court it was an accident. So you'll have your trouble for your pains."

"I will, hey? Well, I'll show you, Ezra Larabee. I'll teach you to come around here bustin' my things up with your old airship! You ought to be ashamed of yourself, a man of your age, trying to fly like a hen or rooster."

"I'm trying for the government prize," said Dick's uncle, weakly.

"Huh! A heap sight chance YOU have of winnin' a prize, flyin' like that!" sneered Mr. Crittenden. "Comin' down in my orchard that way!"

"It was an accident," went on the former army man. "We were making a landing, but we did not intend to come clown just in that spot. We are sorry the tree is broken, but accidents will happen, and—"

"Yes, and them as does 'em must pay for 'em!" exclaimed Hank.

At the mention of money Uncle Ezra looked pained. He looked more so when Hank went on:

"I'll have damages for that tree, that's what I'll have and good damages too. That was my best Baldwin tree—"

"You told us that before," said Larson, as he began to wheel the aeroplane out into an open space where he could get it started again.

"Here, where you takin' that?" demanded Hank, suspiciously.

"We're going to fly back to Dankville," replied Mr. Larson.

"No, you ain't! You ain't goin' t' move that machine until you pay fer the damage to my tree!" insisted Hank, as he took a firmer grasp of the club. "I want ten dollars for what you done to my tree."

"Ten dollars!" grasped Uncle Ezra. "'Tain't wuth half that if it was loaded with apples."

"Well, you'll pay me ten dollars, Ezra Larabee, or you don't take that machine away from here!" insisted the owner of the orchard. "You beat me once in a lawsuit, but you won't again!"

The two had been enemies for many years, Mr. Crittenden insisting that a certain lawsuit, which went against him, had been wrongfully decided in favor of Dick's uncle.

"Well, I won't pay no ten dollars," said Mr. Larabee, firmly, putting his hand in his pocket, as if to resist any attempt to get money from it.

"Ten dollars or you don't take that machine out!" cried Hank. "You're trespassers on my land, too! I could have you arrested for that, as well as suin' ye fer bustin' my tree."

"I'll never pay," said Uncle Ezra. "Come on, Lieutenant, we'll take the airship out in spite of him."

"Oh, you will, eh?" cried Hank. "Well, we'll see about that! I reckoned you'd try some such mean game as that Ezra Larabee, and I'm ready for you. Here, Si and Bill!" he called, and from behind a big tree stepped two stalwart hired men, armed with pitchforks.

"This Ezra Larabee allows he'll not pay for damagin' my tree," explained Hank. "I say he shall, and I don't want you boys t' let him take his contraption away until he forks over ten dollars."

"It ain't worth nigh that sum," began Mr. Larabee. "I'll never—"

"I think, perhaps, you had better pay it to avoid trouble," said the lieutenant. "He has some claim on us."

"Oh, dear!" groaned Uncle Ezra. "More money! This airship business will ruin me. Ten dollars!"

"Not a cent less!" declared Hank.

"Won't you call it eight?" asked the crabbed old miser.

"Ten dollars if you want to take away your machine, and then you can consider yourselves lucky that I don't sue you for trespass. Hand over ten dollars!"

"Never!" declared Ezra Larabee.

"I really think you had better," advised the aviator, and then with a wry face, and much reluctance, Dick's uncle passed over the money.

"Now, you kin go!" cried Hank, "but if I ketch you on my property ag'in you won't git off so easy. You can go back, boys; I won't need you this time," he added grimly.

The hired men departed, and Mr. Crittenden, pocketing the money, watched the lieutenant and Uncle Ezra wheel the biplane out to an open place where a start could be made.

The machine was somewhat damaged, but it could still be operated. The motor, however, was obstinate, and would not start. Hank added insult to injury, at least in the opinion of Uncle Ezra, by laughing at the efforts of the lieutenant. And finally when the motor did consent to "mote," it went so slowly that not enough momentum could be obtained to make the airship rise. It simply rolled slowly over the ground.

"Ha! Ha! That's a fine flyin' machine you've got there!" cried Hank, laughing heartily. "You'd better walk if you're goin' t' git any gov'ment prize!"

"Oh, dry up!" spluttered Uncle Ezra, who was now "real mad" as he admitted later. He and the lieutenant wheeled the machine back to have another try, and this time they were successful in getting up in the air. The aviator circled about and headed for Dankville, the airship having come down about three miles from Uncle Ezra's place.

"Well, you're flyin' that's a fact!" cried Mr. Crittenden, as he looked aloft at them. "But I wouldn't be surprised t' see 'em come smashin' down ag'in any minute," he added pessimistically. "Anyhow, I got ten dollars out of Ezra Larabee!" he concluded, with a chuckle.

Mr. Larabee looked glum when he and the lieutenant got back to the airship shed.

"This is costing me a terrible pile of money!" said the crabbed old man. "A terrible pile! And I reckon you'll have to spend more for fixing her up; won't you?" he asked, in a tone that seemed to indicate he hoped for a negative answer.

"Oh, yes, we'll have to fix her up," said the lieutenant, "and buy a new carburetor, too. You know you promised that."

"Yes, I suppose so," sighed Uncle Ezra. "More money! And that skunk Hank Crittenden got ten dollars out of me! I'll never hear the last of that. I'd rather have landed anywhere but on his land. Oh, this is awful! I wish I'd never gone into it."

"But think of the twenty thousand dollars," said the former army man quickly. It would not do to have his employer get too much discouraged. And the aviator wanted more money—very much more.

The airship was repaired in the next few days, though there was a constant finding of fault on the part of Uncle Ezra. He parted with cash most reluctantly.

However, he had officially made his entry for the government prize, and he could not withdraw now. He must keep on. Lieutenant Larson arranged with one of the army aviators to accompany them on the prospective trip from coast to coast, and finally Larson announced that he was ready to start for New York, where the flight would officially begin.

"Well, Ezra," said his wife, as he climbed into the machine on the day appointed, "I don't like to be a discourager, and throw cold water on you, but I don't reckon I'll ever see you again, Ezra," and she wiped her eyes.

"Oh, pshaw! Of course you'll see me again!" her husband cried. "I'm going to come back with that twenty thousand dollars. And I—I'll buy a new carriage;—that's what I will!"

"That's awful good of you, Ezra," she said. "But I'm not countin' on it. I'm afraid you'll never come back," she sighed.

"Oh, yes, I will!" he declared. "Good-bye!"

They were to pick up the army officer in New York, and so Larson and Uncle Ezra made the first part of the journey alone. They had considerable trouble on the way, having to come down a number of times.

"Say, if she's going to work this way what will happen when we start for San Francisco?" asked Mr. Larabee.

"Oh, it will be all right when I make a few changes in her," the lieutenant said. "And when we have another man aboard she'll ride easier."

"Well, I hope so," murmured Uncle Ezra. "But more changes! Will they—er—cost money?"

"A little."

Uncle Ezra groaned.

However, New York was eventually reached, and after some repairs and changes were made, the airship was taken to the same place where Dick's had started from, and with the army representative aboard, the journey for the Pacific coast was begun. The beginning of the flight was auspicious enough, but if Uncle Ezra could have known all that was before him I am doubtful if he would have gone on.

CHAPTER XXIII

AN IMPROMPTU RACE

"How's she running?"

"Couldn't be better!"

"You're not crowding her though, are you? I mean we can go faster; can't we?"

"Oh, yes, but I think if we average fifty miles an hour for the whole trip, we'll be doing well."

Dick, Paul and Innis were talking together in the small pilot-house of the airship. And it was Dick who made the remark about the speed. They had risen high above New York now, and were headed across the Hudson to the Jersey shore. They would cover the Western part of the Garden State.

"It sure is great!" cried Innis, as he looked down from the height. "If anyone had told me, a year ago, that I'd be doing this, I'd never have believed him."

"Me either!" declared Dick. "But it's the best sport I ever heard about."

"And you sure have got some airship!" declared Larry, admiringly. The young reporter had just finished writing an account of the start, heading his article, "Aboard the Abaris," and, enclosed in a leather holder, had dropped the story from a point near the clouds. The leather cylinder had a small flag attached to it, and as it was dropped down while the airship was shooting across the city, it attracted considerable attention. By means of a glass Larry saw his story picked up, and he felt sure it would reach the paper safely. And he learned, later, such was the case.

"We'd better arrange to divide up the work of running things while we're in the airship," suggested Dick. "We want to have some sort of system."

"That's right," agreed Mr. Vardon. "We shall have to do some sleeping."

"How long do you figure you will take for the trip?" asked Lieutenant McBride, who was making official notes of the manner in which the motor behaved, and of the airship in general.

"Well," answered Dick, "we can make a hundred miles an hour when we're put to it," and he looked at Mr. Vardon for confirmation.

"Yes, that can be done," the aviator said. "But of course we could not keep that up, as the motor would hardly stand it. But fifty miles, on the average, for the entire trip, would be a fair estimate I think."

"And figuring on it being three thousand miles from New York to San Francisco, we could do it in sixty hours of continuous flight," added Dick. "Only of course we'll not have such luck as that."

"No, we've got to make one descent anyhow, about half-way across, to take on more oil and gasolene," Mr. Vardon said. "And we will be very lucky if we don't have to come down but once more on the way. But we may have luck."

"I think we will!" cried Dick.

While the young millionaire was at the wheel, taking the airship higher and higher, and Westward on her journey. Mr. Vardon and Lieutenant McBride arranged a schedule of work, so that each one would have an opportunity of steering.

"And while you're at it," suggested Innis, "I wish you'd arrange a schedule for the cooking. Have I got to do it all?"

"Indeed not," said Dick. "We'll put Paul and Larry to work in the galley."

"Not me!" exclaimed Paul. "I can't even cook water without burning it."

"Get out! Don't you always do your share of the camp cooking when we go off on hikes and practice marches?" objected Innis, to his cadet chum. "Indeed and you'll do your share of it here all right! I'll see to that."

"I guess I'm caught!" admitted Paul.

The start had been made about ten o'clock in the morning, and before noon more than ninety miles had been covered, as registered on the distance gage. This took the party across New Jersey.

They had passed over Newark, and the Orange mountains. The rule against flying over a city had bothered Dick who argued that it would take him much out of his air line, and consume more time if he always had to pick out an unpopulated section.

So the rule was abrogated as far as the aviation association was concerned.

"And if the policemen of any cities we fly over want to take a chance and chase us in an aerial motor cycle, let 'em come!" laughed the young millionaire.

Dinner was served at a height of about eight thousand feet. Dick wanted to get himself and his companions accustomed to great heights, as they would have to fly high over the Rockies. There was some little discomfort, at first, in the rarefied atmosphere, but they soon got used to it, and liked it. Grit, however, suffered considerably, and did not seem to care for aeroplaning. But he was made so much of, and everyone was so fond of, him that he seemed, after a while, to forget his troubles. He wanted to be near Dick all the time.

Mr. Vardon was a veteran aviator, and heights did not bother him. Lieutenant McBride, too, had had considerable experience.

Afternoon found the Abaris over Pennsylvania, which state would require about six hours to cross at the speed of fifty miles every sixty minutes. The captive balloons, and other landmarks, enabled them to keep to their course.

Dick put his craft through several "stunts" to further test its reliability and flexibility. To every one she answered perfectly. The gyroscope stabilizer was particularly effective, and no matter how severe a strain was put on the craft, she either came to an even keel at once when deflected from it, or else did not deviate from it.

"I shall certainly report as to the wisdom of having such an apparatus on every airship the United States uses," declared Lieutenant McBride. "No matter whether Dick Hamilton's craft wins the prize or not,—and I certainly hope he does—the gyroscope must be used."

"I am glad to hear you say so," spoke the inventor, "but I never would have been able to perfect it had it not been for my friend Dick Hamilton."

"Why don't you blush, Dick?" asked Innis, playfully.

"I don't take any credit to myself at all," said the young millionaire.

"Well, I'm going to give it to you," declared the aviator. "From now on the gyroscope stabilizer will be known as the Vardon-Hamilton, and some additional patents I contemplate taking out will be in our joint names."

"Thanks," said Dick, "but I'll accept only on one condition."

"What is that?"

"It is that no money from this invention comes to me. If I win the twenty thousand dollar prize I'll be content."

"What are you going to do with the money?" asked Paul Drew, for Dick really had no need of it.

"I'll build a new gym, at Kentfield," was the reply. "Our present one is too small. We need an indoor baseball cage too."

"Good for you!" cried Innis. "You're a real sport!"

In the evolutions of the airship each one aboard was given a chance to pilot her. He was also allowed to stop and start the machinery, since it could not be told at what moment, in an emergency, someone would have to jump into the breech.

It was about three o'clock in the afternoon, when Dick's ship was nearing the Western borders of Pennsylvania, that Paul, who was looking down through the celluloid floor in the cabin, cried out:

"Something going on down below us, boys!"

All save Innis, who was steering, crowded around the odd window.

"Why, there's an airship meet going on down there," said Dick. "Look, there are a lot of monoplanes and some biplanes."

"Let's go down a bit and salute them," suggested Larry.

"Down she is!" cried Innis, as he pulled over the lever of the deflecting rudder. "Say when, Dick."

"Oh, keep her up about two thousand feet. We don't want to interfere with any of their evolutions."

But the advent of the Abaris seemed welcomed by the other airships that were taking part in the evolutions below. Two of them, which had been flying high, at once pointed their noses upward, and raced forward to get in line with Dick's craft.

"They're going to race us!" Paul shouted.

"Come on, Dick, now's your chance!"

"Shall I?" the young millionaire asked of Mr. Vardon.

"Yes, go ahead. Let's see what we can do to them. Though they are probably much swifter than we are."

"Take the wheel, Dick!" cried Innis. "I want to see you beat 'em."

The implied challenge was at once accepted, and in another moment the impromptu race was under way.

CHAPTER XXIV

GRIT'S GRIP

Two large biplanes were in the race with Dick Hamilton's airship. They were of the latest type, as could be noted by the young millionaire, and were swift craft. They had come up from behind, on a long, upward slant, and were now about in line with each other, and on a par with the Abaris, though considerably below her.

"Say, look at that crowd of people!" exclaimed Paul, as he stood at the side of Dick who was at the wheel. The cadet was ready to lend any assistance that might be needed in working the airship.

"Yes, there is quite a bunch," observed Dick, as he opened the gasolene throttle a little wider, and took a quick glance down through the celluloid bull's-eye in the floor of the cabin. "It's a big meet."

They were flying over a big aviation park, that Mr. Vardon at once recognized as one in which he had given several exhibitions.

"This is quite a meet, all right," the aviator remarked as he noted at least ten machines in the air at one time. There were mono and biplanes, but only two of the latter were near enough to Dick's machine to engage in the impromptu race with it.

"How are we coming on?" asked Paul.

"Holding our own," answered the young millionaire. "I haven't started to speed yet. I'm waiting to see what those fellows are going to do."

The latter, however, were evidently also hanging back trying to "get a line" on the performance of the big craft. The pilots of the lower biplanes could, very likely, tell by the size of the Abaris that she was no ordinary airship, and, in all probability, they had read of her, and of the try for the prize. For Larry Dexter made a good press agent, and had written many a story of Dick's plans.

"Now they're coming on," cried Dick, as he saw one of the lower machines dart ahead of the other. "He's trying to get me to sprint, I guess."

"Why don't you try it now?" suggested Mr. Vardon. "We'll soon be at the limits of the aviation field, and I doubt if these machines will be allowed to go beyond it. So, if you want to beat them in a race now is your time to speed up."

"Here she goes!" cried Dick, as he opened wider the gasolene throttle.

In an instant the big craft shot ahead, fairly roaring through the air. The closed cabin, however, kept the pressure of wind from the occupants, or they might not have been able to stand it, for the gage outside registered a resistance of many pounds to the square inch.

It was an odd race. There were no cheering spectators to urge on the contestants by shouts and cheers, though doubtless those who were witnessing the evolutions of the aircraft, before Dick's advent on the scene, were using their voices to good advantage. But the birdmen were too high up to hear them.

Nor could the excited calls, if there were any such, from the two rivals of our hero be heard. There were two men in each of the competing biplanes, and they were doing their best to win.

It must have been an inspiring sight from below, for Dick's craft was so large that it showed up well, and the white canvas planes of the others, as well as those of the Abaris, stood out in bold contrast to the blue of the sky.

"We're doing ninety an hour!" called Dick, after a glance at the speed gage, while his companions were looking down at the craft below.

"Pretty nearly the limit," remarked Mr. Vardon. "If you can reach a hundred, Dick, do it. I don't believe those fellows can come near that."

"They're falling behind now," observed Paul. "Go to it, Dick, old man!"

The young millionaire pulled open the gasolene throttle to the full limit and set the sparker to contact at the best advantage. The result was at once apparent. The aircraft shot ahead in a wonderful fashion. The others evidently put on full speed, for they, also, made a little spurt.

Then it was "all over but the shouting," as Larry said. Dick's machine swept on and soon distanced the others.

"I've got to get back a story of this!" cried Larry. "It will be good reading for those who buy the Leader."

"But how are you going to do it?" asked Paul. "You can't send back a story now, and we'd have to make a descent to use the wireless," Dick's craft being so fitted up.

"I'll just write a little note, telling the editor to get the story from the Associated Press correspondent who is covering this meet," Larry answered. "All they need in the

Leader office is a 'tip.' They'll do the rest. But I'll just give them a few pointers as to how things went on here."

He hastily dashed off a story and enclosed it in one of several leather cylinders he had provided for this purpose. Each one had a sort of miniature parachute connected to it, and a flag to attract attention as it shot down.

Enclosing his story in one of these Larry dropped it, as he had done before, trusting that it would be picked up and forwarded. The plan always worked well.

The leather messenger fell on the aviation field, and our friends had the satisfaction of seeing several men running to pick it up, so Larry knew his plan would be successful.

The Abaris was now speeding along at the top notch, and for a few minutes Dick allowed her to soar through the air in this fashion. And then, having some regard for his engines, he cut down the gasolene, and slowed up.

"No use tearing her heart out," he remarked.

"There's time enough to rush on the last lap. I wonder if we'll have a race at the end?"

"I shouldn't be surprised," Mr. Vardon answered. "A number of celebrated aviators are planning to compete for this prize, and some may already be on the way across the continent ahead of us."

"Then there's your Uncle Ezra," put in Paul.

"Poor Uncle Ezra," spoke Dick, musingly. "He certainly has treated me mean, at times, but I can't help feeling sorry for him. Every time he has to buy five gallons of gasolene, or some oil, he'll imagine he's getting ready to go to the poorhouse. He certainly was not cut out for an aviator, and I certainly was surprised when he built that airship."

"He's being used by that fellow Larson, I'm sure of that," declared Mr. Vardon. "Your Uncle Ezra has fallen into the hands of a scoundrel, Dick."

"Well, I'm sorry for that, of course," said the young millionaire, "but, do you know, I think it will do Uncle Ezra good to lose some of his money. He's got more than he needs, and he can afford to spend some on aviation. Someone, at least the workmen, and those who sell materials and supplies, will get the benefit of it."

The aircraft was now going along at about her usual speed of fifty miles an hour. The aviation park had been left behind, and they were now flying along at a comparatively low altitude.

"Better go up a little," suggested Mr. Vardon. "It will be dark shortly, and we don't want to run into a mountain in the night."

Dick tilted the elevating rudder and the craft lifted herself into the air, soaring upward.

"Here, Innis, you take the wheel now, it's your turn," called our hero, a little later. "Straighten her out and keep her on a level keel. It's my turn to get supper."

"And give us plenty, if you don't mind," begged the stout cadet, who took his chum's place in the pilot house. "This upper atmosphere seems to give me an appetite."

"I never saw you without it, Innis," laughed Paul.

"Come on out on the deck, for a breath of air before we start to cook," suggested Larry. "We can get a fine view of the sunset there."

The open deck, in the rear of the cabin, did indeed offer a gorgeous view of the setting sun, which was sinking to rest in a bank of golden, green and purple clouds.

"I'll go out, too," said Lieutenant McBride. "I am supposed to make some meteorological observations while I am on this trip, and it is high time I began."

And so, with the exception of Innis, who would have his turn later, and Mr. Vardon, who wanted to look over the machinery, for possible heated bearings, all went out on the railed deck. Grit, the bulldog, followed closely on the heels of Dick.

"Be careful, old man," said the young millionaire to his pet. "There's no rail close to the deck, you know, and you may slip overboard."

They stood for a few moments viewing the scene while thus flying along through the air. The colors of the sunset were constantly changing, becoming every moment more gorgeous.

Suddenly there was a swerve to the airship, and it tilted sharply to one side.

"Look out!" cried Dick, as he grasped the protecting railing, an example followed by all. "What's up?"

"We're falling!" shouted Paul.

"No, it's just an air pocket," was the opinion of Lieutenant McBride. "We'll be all right in another moment."

They were, but before that Grit, taken unawares, had slid unwillingly to the edge of the open deck.

"Look out for him!" shouted Dick, making a grab for his pet.

But he was too late. The deck was smooth, and the bulldog could get no grip on it. In another instant he had toppled over the edge of the platform, rolling under the lowest of the guard rails.

"There he goes!" cried Paul.

Dick gave a gasp of despair. Grit let out a howl of fear.

And then, as Larry Dexter leaned over the side, he gave a cry of surprise.

"Look!" he shouted. "Grit's caught by a rope and he's hanging there by his teeth!"

And, as Dick looked, he saw a strange sight. Trailing over the side of the airship deck was a piece of rope, that had become loosed. And, in his fall, Grit had caught hold of this in his strong jaws. To this he clung like grim death, his grip alone keeping him from falling into space.

CHAPTER XXV

A FORCED LANDING

"Hold on there, old boy! Don't let go!" begged Dick of his pet, who swung to and fro, dangling like some grotesque pendulum over the side of the airship. "Hold on, Grit!"

And Grit held on, you may be sure of that. His jaws were made for just that purpose. The dog made queer gurgling noises in his throat, for he dare not open his mouth to bark. Probably he knew just what sort of death would await him if he dropped into the vast space below him.

"How we going to get him up?" asked Larry.

"I'll show you!" cried Dick, as he stretched out at full length on the deck, and made his way to the edge where his head and shoulders projected over the dizzying space. The airship was still rushing on.

"Grab his legs—somebody!" exclaimed Paul. "I'll sit on you, Dick!"

"That's right! Anchor me down, old man!" Dick cried. "I'm going to get Grit!"

"Are you going to make a landing to save him?" asked Larry.

"No, though I would if I had to," Dick replied. "I'm just going to haul him up by the rope. Keep a good hold, old boy!" he encouraged his pet, and Grit gurgled his answer.

And then Dick, leaning over the edge of the deck, while Paul sat on his backward-stretched legs to hold him in place, hauled up the bulldog hand over hand, by means of the rope the intelligent animal had so fortunately grasped.

Inch by inch Grit was raised until Larry, who had come to the edge to help Dick, reached out, and helped to haul the dog in.

"There he is!" cried Dick, as he slid back.

"Well, old boy, you had a close call!"

Grit let go the rope and barked. And then a strange fit of trembling seized him. It was the first time he had ever showed fear. He never ventured near the edge of the deck again, always taking a position as near the centre as possible, and lying down at full length, to prevent any danger of sliding off. And he never went out on the deck unless

Dick went also, feeling, I suppose, that he wanted his master near in case of accidents.

"Say, that was some little excitement," remarked the young millionaire, as he wiped the beads of perspiration from his forehead. "I thought poor old Grit was sure a goner."

"It did look so," admitted Paul. "He's an intelligent beast, all right."

"Takes after me," laughed Dick. "Well, let's see how Innis made out while we were at the rescue."

"I was all ready to send her down quick, if you'd given the word," said the cadet in the pilot house, when the party went inside the cabin.

"But she's still on her course," he added, after a glance at the compass.

"I'm glad we didn't have to go down," Dick remarked. "As we only have two landings we can make I want to save my reserve until we are actually forced to use it. I wonder about where we are, anyhow? Let's make a calculation."

By figuring out the rate of speed, and comparing the elapsed time, and then by figuring on a scale map, it was estimated, as dusk settled down, that they were about on the border line between Pennsylvania and Ohio.

"We'll cross the state of Ohio tonight," spoke Dick, "and by morning we ought to be in Indiana. Not so bad, considering that we haven't really pushed the machine to the limit yet, except in that little brush with the other airships."

"Yes, we are doing very well," said Mr. Vardon. "I wonder how some of our competitors are making out? I'd like to get some news of them."

"So would I," went on Dick. "Particularly my Uncle Ezra."

Had he but known it, Mr. Larabee, in his airship with Larson and the army man, was following close after him. For really the big biplane, with the mercury stabilizers, which Larson had constructed, was a fine craft, and capable. That Larson had cheated Mr. Larabee out of considerable money in the building had nothing to do with the working of the apparatus. But of Uncle Ezra and his aircraft more later.

"We'll get some news the first landing we make," suggested Lieutenant McBride.

"Well, I would like to get news all right," admitted Dick. "But I don't want to go down until I have to. Now for supper. Anything you fellows would like, especially?"

"Green turtle soup for mine!" sung out Larry.

"I'll have pickled eels' feet," laughed Innis, who had relinquished the wheel to Mr. Vardon. "Wait a bit, Dick, and I'll drop a line overboard and catch a few."

"And I'll see if I can't shoot a mock turtle," came from Paul.

"Nothing but roast turkey for mine," insisted Lieutenant McBride. "But I guess we'll have to compromise on capsule soup and condensed sandwiches."

"Oh, I can give you canned chicken," promised the young millionaire, "and perhaps I can make it hot for you."

"Not too much tabasco sauce though, the way you dosed up the stuff for the last Freshman dinner!" objected Paul. "I ate some of that by mistake, and I drank nothing but iced water for a week after."

"That's right—it was a hot old time!" cried Dick, with a laugh at the recollection.

As space was rather limited on board the airship, no ice could be carried, and, in consequence no fresh meats were available except for the first few hours of travel. Of course, when a landing was to be made, another limited supply could be laid in, but, with only two descents to earth allowed, this would not help much.

However, as the trip was going to be a comparatively short one, no one minded the deprivation from the usual bountiful meals that, somehow, one seemed to associate with the young millionaire.

A good supply of "capsule" food was carried. In making up his larder Dick had consulted Lieutenant McBride, who had given him a list of the highly nutritious and condensed food used in the army.

While such food was not the most appetizing in the world, it could be carried in a small space, was easily prepared, and would sustain life, and provide working energy, fully as long as the more elaborate dishes, which contain a large amount of waste materials.

Soon the electric stove was aglow, and on it Dick got up a tasty supper. Innis insisted on helping his chum, though it was Dick's turn to play cook.

"You just can't keep out of the kitchen; can you?" asked Dick, of the stout cadet. "You always want to be around where eating is going on."

"Well, the only way to be sure of a thing, is to do it yourself," said Innis. "I would hate to have this fine appetite of mine go to waste."

It was quite dark when they sat at supper, for some slight defect manifested itself in one of the small motors just as they were about to eat, and it had to be repaired at once.

But, gathered about the folding table, with the electric lights aglow overhead, there was little indication among the party of aviators that they were in one of the most modern of skycraft, sailing a mile above the earth, and shooting along at fifty miles an hour. So easy was the motion of the Abaris, and so evenly and smoothly did she glide along, due to the automatic action of the gyroscope stabilizer, that it really seemed as if they were standing still—floating between heaven and earth.

Of course there was the subdued hum of the great propellers outside, and the throb of the powerful gasolene motor, but that was all that gave an idea of the immense force contained in the airship.

From time to time Lieutenant McBride made notes for future use. He had to report officially to the war department just how this type of airship behaved under any and all circumstances. Then, too, he was interested personally, for he had taken up aviation with great enthusiasm, and as there were not many army men in it, so far, he stood a good chance for advancement.

"The possibilities of aeroplanes in time of war are only beginning to be understood," he said. "Of course there has been a lot of foolish talk about them, and probably they will not be capable of doing all that has been claimed for them, as yet. But they will be of immense value for scouting purposes, if for nothing else. In rugged and mountainous countries, an aviator will be under no difficulties at all, and can, by hovering over the enemy's camp, get an idea of the defenses, and report back.

"Thus it will be possible to map out a plan of attack with every chance of success. There will be no time lost, and lives may be saved from useless exposure."

"Do you think airships will ever carry light artillery, or drop bombs on an enemy?" asked Dick.

"Well, you could carry small artillery aboard here if you didn't have so much company," answered the army man. "It is all a question of weight and size. However,

I believe, for the present, the most valuable aid airships will render will be in the way of scouting. But I don't want to see a war just for the sake of using our airships. Though it is well to be prepared to take advantage of their peculiar usefulness."

After supper they prepared to spend their first night aboard the airship on her prize-winning attempt. They decided to cut down the speed a little.

"Not that there's much danger of hitting anything," Dick explained, "though possibly Uncle Ezra and Larson might come up behind and crash into us. But at slower speed the machinery is not so strained, and there is less likelihood of an accident."

"That's right," agreed Mr. Vardon. "And an accident at night, especially when most of us are asleep, is not so easily handled as when it occurs in daylight. So slow her down, Dick."

The motor was set to take them along at thirty miles an hour, and they descended until they were fifteen hundred feet above the earth, so in case of the Abaris becoming crippled, she would not have to spend much time in making a landing.

Everything was well looked to, and then, with Dick and Mr. Vardon taking the first watch, the others turned in. And they were so tired from the rather nervous excitement of the day of the start, that they were soon asleep. Dick and the aviator took turns at the wheel, and attended to the necessary adjustments of the various machines.

It might seem strange for anyone to sleep aboard a moving airship, but, the truth of the matter was, that our friends were realty worn out with nervous exhaustion. They had tired themselves out, not only physically, but mentally, and sleep was really forced on them. Otherwise they might not have slumbered at all.

It was shortly past midnight when Dick, who, in spite of his attempts to keep awake, had partly dozed off, was suddenly aroused by a howl from Grit.

"What—what's the matter, old boy?" he asked. "In trouble again?"

There came another and louder howl. "Where is he?" asked Mr. Vardon, looking in from the pilot-house.

"I can't see him," Dick answered. "Can he be out on deck?"

A moment later there was a flash as of lightning, within the cabin, and Grit mingled his howls and barks as though in great pain.

"Something's wrong!" cried the aviator. "Look about, Dick, I can't leave the wheel. We seem to be going down!"

The young millionaire sprang up and leaped toward the place where he had heard Grit howling. The next moment Dick laughed in a relieved fashion.

"Where are those rubber gloves?" he asked.

"Rubber gloves?" repeated Mr. Vardon.

"Yes. Grit has gotten tangled up in the little dynamo that runs the headlight, and he's short-circuited. He can stand more of a shock than I can. I want to get him off the contacts. Where are the gloves?"

The aviator directed Dick to where the insulating gauntlets were kept, and in another moment Grit was pulled away from the contact. He had been unable to move himself, just as when one grasps the handles of a galvanic battery the muscles become so bound as to be incapable of motion.

Fortunately the current, while it made Grit practically helpless, for the time, was not strong enough to burn, or otherwise injure him. He gave a howl of protest at the accident, as Dick released him, and shuffled off to his kennel, after fawning on his master.

"One of the wires has some of the insulation off—that's what caused the trouble," Dick explained. "I'll wind some tape on it until we have time to put in a new conductor."

"Grit seems to be getting the worst end of it this trip," said Paul, who had been awakened by the commotion.

"Yes, he isn't much used to airships," agreed Dick. "But you'd better turn in, Paul. You've got an hour yet before it's your turn at the wheel."

"Oh, better let me have it now. I'm awake, and I can't get to sleep again. Turn in yourself."

Which Dick was glad enough to do, as he was quite tired. The remainder of the night passed without incident, and when morning came the airship was put at her former speed, fifty miles an hour. That may not sound very fast, but it must be remembered that this rate had to be kept up for sixty hours straight, perhaps.

After breakfast the wire that had shocked Grit was renewed, and then some observations were taken to determine their position. It was calculated they were about halfway across Indiana by noon.

The afternoon was slowly waning, and they were preparing for their second night of the prize trip, congratulating themselves that they had not yet been forced to descend.

Suddenly Larry, who was at the wheel, uttered a cry of alarm.

"Something's wrong!" he shouted. "I can't steer her on the course any longer. She's heading North instead of West."

Dick and Mr. Vardon rushed to the pilot-house. A glance at the compass confirmed Larry's statement. The aviator himself took the wheel, but it was impossible to head the craft West. She pointed due North.

"The horizontal rudder is out of gear!" cried Dick.

"Yes, and we'll have to go down to fix it," said Mr. Vardon, after a quick inspection. "Boys, we've got to make our first landing! It's too bad, but it might be worse."

CHAPTER XXVI

ON LAKE MICHIGAN

Unsuccessfully they tried to make repairs to the horizontal rudder without going down, but it was not to be. The airship was being sent farther and farther along on a Northern course, taking her far out of her way. And more time and distance might thus be lost than by descending, making repairs, and going on again.

"Well, I did hope we'd cover at least half the trip before we had to go down," Dick said, and his tone was regretful. "Try once more and see if we can't get her back on the course."

But the horizontal guide—by which I mean the apparatus that sent the craft to left or right—was hopelessly jammed. To try to force it might mean a permanent break.

"Take her down," Dick finally gave the order, as captain. "What sort of a landing-place is below us?"

"We're too far up to see," said Mr. Vardon.

"And I hope we have the luck to be above open country. We can't go to left or right except in the smallest degree, so we'll have to land wherever Fate disposes. We are all right on going up or down, but not otherwise."

The vertical rudder was now depressed, and on a long slant Dick's airship was sent down. Lower and lower she glided, and soon an indistinct mass appeared. It was almost dusk, and no details could be made out. Then, as she went lower what appeared to be a gray cloud showed.

"There's a bank of fog below us," declared Paul.

"Or else it's the smoke of Pittsburg," said Innis.

"We left Pittsburg behind long ago," Larry returned. "Why!" he cried, as the gray foglike mass became more distinct. "That's water—that's what it is!"

"Water!" exclaimed Dick. "Can we have gone in the wrong direction, and be back over the Atlantic?"

"Or the Pacific?" suggested Larry with a laugh.

"No such good luck as that! We haven't had time to cross the continent yet," declared Dick. "But what water can it be?"

"Oh, some small lake," spoke Paul.

"It isn't a small lake—it's a big one—an inland sea," was Dick's opinion, as they settled lower and lower.

"It's Lake Michigan, that's what it is!" shouted Larry, after a quick glance at the map. "Fellows, we're over Lake Michigan!"

"And we're going to be IN it—or on it—in a little while, I'm thinking," Lieutenant McBride said, grimly. "Are you ready for a bath?"

"There won't be any trouble about that," answered Dick. "The hydroplanes will take care of us. I only hope it isn't too rough to make a safe landing."

Paul took a telescope from the rack, and, going out on the deck, looked down. The next moment he reported:

"It's fairly calm. Just a little swell on."

"Then we'd better get ready to lower the hydroplanes," went on Dick, with a look at the aviator.

"That's the best thing to do," decided Mr. Vardon. "We'll see how they'll work in big water."

The hydroplanes, which were attached to the airship near the points where the starting wheels were made fast, could be lowered into place by means of levers in the cabin. The hydroplanes were really water-tight hollow boxes, large and buoyant enough to sustain the airship on the surface of the water. They could be lowered to a point where they were beneath the bicycle wheels, and were fitted with toggle-jointed springs to take up the shock.

Lieutenant McBride took out his watch, and with pad and pencil prepared to note the exact moment when the airship should reach the surface of the lake.

"I shall have to take official notice of this," he said. "It constitutes your first landing, though perhaps it would be more correct to call it a watering. As soon as you are afloat, your elapsed time will begin, and it will count until you are in the air again. You will probably be some time making repairs."

"No longer than we can help," said Dick. "I don't want Uncle Ezra, or anybody else, to get ahead of me."

Down and down sank the Abaris, on her first descent from the cloud-land since her auspicious start. But, as Dick admitted, it might be worse. The accident itself was a comparatively slight one.

"Get ready, everybody!" called Mr. Vardon, as he saw that, in a few seconds more, they would be on the surface of the water.

"Do you fear something will go wrong?" asked Larry, quickly.

"Well, we've never tried the hydroplanes in rough water, and there is always the chance for an accident. Stand out where you can jump, if you have to," he directed.

Lieutenant McBride was standing with his watch out, ready to note the exact second of landing. He knew he must be officially correct, though he would give Dick every possible chance and favor.

"Here we go!" came the cry from the aviator. "Only a few seconds now!"

They could plainly see the heaving waters of the big lake. Fortunately it was comparatively calm, though once she had landed the airship could stand some rough weather afloat.

Splash! went the hydroplanes into the water. The springs took up the shock and strain, and the next moment Dick's craft was floating easily on the great lake. The landing had been made without an accident to mar it.

"Good!" cried Lieutenant McBride, as he jotted down the time. "Do you know how long you have been, so far, Dick, on the trip?"

"How long?"

"Just thirty-five hours, four minutes and eight seconds!" was the answer.

"Over half the estimated time gone, and we re only a third of the way there!" exclaimed the young millionaire. "I'm afraid we aren't going to do it, Mr. Vardon."

"Well, I'm not going to give up yet," the aviator answered, grimly. "This is only a start. We haven't used half our speed, and when we get closer to the finish we can go a hundred and twenty-five miles an hour if we have to—for a spurt, at any rate. No, I'm not giving up."

"Neither am I," declared Dick, for he was not of the quitting sort.

Floating on the surface of Lake Michigan was like being on the ocean, for they were out of sight of land, and there were no water craft in view. The Abaris seemed to have the lake to herself, though doubtless beyond the wall of the slight haze that hemmed her in there were other vessels.

"Well, now to see what the trouble is," suggested Dick. "It must be somewhere in the connecting joints of the levers, for the rudder itself seems to be all right."

"But we'd better begin out there and make sure," suggested Mr. Vardon. He pointed to the rudder, which projected some distance back of the stern of the aircraft.

"How you going to get at it to inspect it?" asked Paul. "It isn't as if we were on solid ground."

"And no one has long enough a reach to stretch to it from the deck," added Innis.

"You forget our collapsible lifeboat," Dick answered. One of those useful craft was aboard the airship. It could be inflated with air, and would sustain a considerable weight.

"I'll go out in that and see what's the trouble," Dick went on. "It will tell us where we've got to begin."

"Perhaps we had better wait until morning," suggested Lieutenant McBride. "It is fast getting dark, and you can do much better work in daylight. Besides, you are not pressed for time, as your stay here will not count against you. I think you had better wait until morning."

"And stay here all night?" asked Dick.

"I think so. You have proved that your hydroplanes are all right. Why not rest on the surface of the lake until morning? You can't anchor, it is true, but you can use a drag, and there seems to be no wind, so you will not be blown ashore. Besides, you can, to a certain extent, control yourself with the propellers."

"I think we will wait then," decided the young millionaire captain. "As you say we can make a drag anchor to keep us from drifting too much."

By means of a long rope a drag anchor was tossed out at the stern of the aircraft. This would serve to hold her back. Then, as nothing further could be done, preparations were made for supper.

"Well, this aeroplaning has its ups and downs," said Paul, with a laugh, as he sat at table. "Last night we were eating up in the air, and now we're on the water."

"And it's lucky we're not IN the water!" exclaimed Innis. "Regular Hamilton luck, I call it."

"No, it's Vardon luck," Dick insisted. "He planned the hydroplanes that made it possible."

Lights were set aglow to show the position of the craft on the water.

"We don't want to be run down in the night," Dick said, as he noted the red and green side lights as well as the white ones at bow and stern. For, in the water, the Abaris was subject to the same rules as were other lake craft. It was only when in the air that she was largely a law unto herself.

The night passed quietly enough, though it came on to blow a little toward morning. But the drag anchor worked well.

"And now for the repairs," cried Dick, after breakfast, as he and his chums got out the collapsible boat. It was blown up, and in it Dick and Mr. Vardon paddled out to the stern rudders.

They were examining the universal joint, by which the apparatus was deflected when Dick suddenly became aware of a wet feeling about his feet, and a sinking feeling beneath him. He looked down, and found that the boat, in which he and Mr. Vardon were standing, was going down. Already it was half filled with water.

"More trouble!" cried Dick. "I guess we'll have to swim for it!"

CHAPTER XXVII

A HOWLING GALE

There was no doubt about it. The little craft was going down. Later it was learned that a leaky valve had allowed the air to escape, and a break in the boat's rubber sides had let in the water.

"Come on!" cried Dick. "Overboard, Mr. Vardon!"

There was really little danger, as both of them could swim, though if they did not jump out they might be carried down with the boat.

So, overboard went Dick and his aviator. The collapsible boat sank with the downward impulse given it when they leaped out, but as it was moored to the airship by a cable it could be recovered.

"Say, what is this—a swimming race?" asked Paul, as he tossed Dick a rope, a like service being performed for Mr. Vardon by Innis.

"Looks like it—doesn't it?" agreed the young millionaire. "I should have tested that boat before we went out in it," he added, as he clambered up, Grit frisking and barking about him in delight.

"Yes, that's where we made the mistake," agreed Mr. Vardon. "That rubber must have been cut as it was packed away. Well, we can easily mend it, so no great harm is done."

By means of the cable, the sunken boat was pulled to the airship, and when the water was allowed to run out it was hauled aboard. Then it was examined, the leak found, and the craft was placed out in the sun to dry, after which it could be mended.

"Well, we can't do anything but wait," said Dick, after he had changed into dry garments. "The break is out on that part of the rudder that's over the water. We can't reach it without the boat."

"Then, while we're waiting let's have a swim," proposed Paul. "It will do us all good."

"And then we can do some fishing," added Innis. "I'd like some nice broiled fish. Did you bring any tackle along, Dick?"

"No, I'm sorry to say I didn't."

"Then I'll have to rig up some. I'll use some cold canned chicken for bait."

"What about a hook?" asked Lieutenant McBride, with a smile.

"Well, anybody who can build an airship ought to be able to make a fish hook. I'm going to call on Dick for that," went on Innis.

"I guess I can file you out one from a bit of steel wire," answered the young millionaire.

This was done, after some little labor, and with several of the improvised barbs, and bait from some of the canned goods, a fishing party was organized. There was plenty of string, and for leaders, so that the fish would not bite off the hooks, Innis used some spare banjo strings. He had brought his instrument along with him.

The swim was much enjoyed, for the day was warm. The young aviators sported around in the cool waters of the lake, and several little spurting races were "pulled off," to use a sporting term.

I cannot say that the fishing was very successful. A few were caught, but I imagine the bait used was not just proper. It is difficult to get canned chicken to stick on a hook, unless you use a piece of gristle. But some good specimens were caught, and were served for dinner, being fried on the electric stove.

All this while the airship floated tranquilly on the surface of the lake. Several vessels came near, attracted by the strange sight of Dick's craft, but, by means of a megaphone they were kindly asked not to approach too near, as the least contact with one of the heavier craft would damage the Abaris. Through the captain of one craft Dick sent a message to his father, and Larry a story to his paper.

"Well, I think that boat must be dry enough to mend now," said Dick, some time after dinner. "We don't want to spend another night here if we can help it."

"No, for the weather might not always be as calm as it is now. The barometer is falling, and that means a storm, sooner or later," spoke Mr. Vardon. "And these lake storms can be pretty had when they try."

It was found that the collapsible boat was dry enough to patch up, and by means of a rubber cement the hole in the side was closed.

The leaky intake valve was also repaired, and then, when the peculiar craft was blown up and tested, it was found to be all right.

"Now we'll have another try at fixing that rudder," said Dick, as he and the aviator started once more to paddle to the stern of the aircraft.

This time all went well. No water came in the rubber boat, and by standing up in it the two were able to learn the cause of the trouble with the rudder.

It was simple enough—a broken bolt making it impossible to turn it in a certain direction. As Dick had plenty of spare parts aboard, a new bolt was soon substituted for the fractured one, and then they were ready to proceed again.

"I've a suggestion to make," said Lieutenant McBride, when Dick was about to give the word to mount into the air again.

"What is it?" asked the young millionaire.

"Why not try your boat over the water? While it is not exactly a hydroplane, yet it has those attachments, and you can probably skim over the surface of the water as well as float on it. And that might come in useful in winning the prize.

"Of course the conditions call for an air flight from New York to San Francisco, but I believe, in case of emergency, a short water trip would not count against you? And you might have to make it some time."

"I'll see what we can do, at any rate," decided Dick. "We will probably never get a better chance than this. Come on, boys! We'll see how our hydroplanes act!" he called.

The only thing that was necessary to do was to start the motor that operated the propellers. The aircraft was at this time resting easily on the surface of Lake Michigan.

She would be driven forward by the propellers beating on the air, exactly as a sailboat it aided by the wind. Only, in her case, the Abaris would furnish her own motive power.

In anticipation of some time having to navigate on the water, a small auxiliary rudder had been attached to Dick's craft. This rudder went down into the water, and would be used in steering in conjunction with those used when she was in the air.

This wooden rudder was now dropped into the water, tested, and found to answer properly to the lever which, in the pilot-house, controlled it by means of wire ropes.

"Well, let her go!" cried Dick, "and we'll see what sort of luck we'll have."

"Which way?" asked Mr. Vardon, who was at the wheel.

"Why not head for Chicago?" suggested Lieutenant McBride. "We can't be a great way from there, according to the map, and that would be a good place to make the new start from."

"I think it would be," agreed Dick, "if that would be covering the conditions of the contest."

"Well, you can easily travel back enough to make up any shortage in miles," the army man went on. "You still have plenty of time."

So this was agreed to, and, after a look over the craft to make sure there were no defects, Mr. Vardon pulled over the lever of the starting motor.

With a hum and a buzz, the propellers started, and this time the Abaris shot forward on the surface of the water, instead of up into the air.

"She's going!" cried Paul.

"She sure is doing it!" yelled Innis.

"Yes, I think she's as successful on the waves as he was in the clouds," agreed Dick, as he looked at a speed-measuring gage. "We're hitting up forty miles an hour right now."

"And that's good speed for a craft of this size in the water, or, rather, on top of the water," declared Lieutenant McBride.

For a hydroplane craft, as you probably know, does not go through the water as a motor-boat does. A regular hydroplane is fitted with a series of graduated steps, and the front of the boat rises as it skims over the water. But all hydroplane craft are designed to slip over the surface of the water, and not to cleave through it. And it was the former that Dick's craft was doing.

Faster and faster speed was attained, until there could be no question about the second success of the young millionaire's airship. If ever occasion should require that he take to the water, in an emergency, it could be done.

"And now for Chicago!" Dick cried, when several hours had been spent in maneuvering about, each member of the party taking turns at steering. "And I think we'll go up in the air for that trip," he added.

"There's an aero club in the outskirts of Chicago," explained Lieutenant McBride. "I am a member of it, and I think we could make a call there. It would not be necessary to cross the city, and of course we will not land."

It was agreed that this would be a good plan, and Dick, taking the wheel, sent his craft ahead on the lake at fast speed.

"Here we go up!" he suddenly cried. Then, yanking over the lever of the elevating rudder, he sent the Abaris aloft. The rudder for sideway steering worked perfectly, now that repairs had been made.

Up, up into the air soared the big biplane, and from the lake she had left came a blast of saluting whistles from the water-craft that thus paid tribute to a sister vessel.

During the wait on the water Dick had purchased from a passing steamer a supply of gasolene and oil.

"Now we'll have enough so we won't have to land to take on any more," he said. "Our provisions are holding out well, and if nothing happens we can make the trip from here to San Francisco without stop."

"But we still have one landing to our credit if we need it," said Paul.

"Oh, yes, but I hope we don't have to use it," went on Dick. "It will be so much more to our credit if we don't."

The supposition that they were not far from Chicago proved correct, for when they had arisen above the mist that suddenly spread over Lake Michigan, they saw, in the distance, the Windy City.

A course was laid to circle about it, and not cross it, as that might complicate matters, and a little later they were within view of the aviation grounds, of which club Lieutenant McBride was a member.

He had said there might be a meet in progress, and this proved to be so. A number of biplanes and monoplanes were circling about, and the big crowd in attendance leaped to its feet in astonishment at the sight of the young millionaire's new and powerful craft.

It was not the intention of Dick and his chums to stop and make a landing, but they wanted to get some news of other competing craft which might be trying for the big prize. Accordingly a plan was evolved by which this could be done.

The lieutenant wrote out a brief account of their trip, telling of the stop, and to this Larry added a request that, after it had been read, it might be telegraphed to his paper. Then information was asked for in regard to aerial matters.

"But how are we going to get information from them?" asked Paul. "We can't get our wireless to working, we can't hear them, even with megaphones, wig-wagging won't do, and we're not going to land."

"I've asked them to send up a bunch of toy balloons, carrying any message they can send us," the lieutenant said. "I think we can manipulate our craft so as to grab some of the balloons as they float upward. I've seen it done."

Little time was lost over this. The message was dropped down in one of Larry's leather cylinders. It was seen to be picked up and while Dick and his friends circled about above the aviation grounds their note was read. An answer was hastily prepared to be sent up as Lieutenant McBride had suggested.

Meanwhile a number of the other aeroplanes whizzed past, close to Dick's.

"I hope they don't come so close that they'll collide with us," murmured the young millionaire. But the pilots were skillful. They tried to shout what were probably congratulations, or questions, at the trans-continental party, but the motors of the small biplanes made such a racket it was impossible to hear.

"Here come the balloons!" cried Dick, as he saw a group tied together floating upward. "Now to get them! You'd better handle her, Mr. Vardon."

"No, you do it, Dick. I'll stand out on deck and try to grab them."

"We can all reach from windows," suggested Paul, for there were windows in the cabin.

Dick was so successful in maneuvering his craft that Mr. Vardon had no trouble at all in catching the message-carrying toy balloons. The note was brief. It conveyed the greeting of the aero-club, and stated that a number of competing craft were on their way west.

"The Larabee leads, according to last reports," read Innis.

"That must be Uncle Ezra's machine," murmured Dick. "He's right after us. Well, we'd better get on our course again."

"I think so," agreed Mr. Vardon. The Abaris was sent in a Westerly direction once more, and those aboard settled down to what they hoped would be the last "lap" of the big race.

But matters were not destined to be as easy and comfortable as they hoped for. Soon after supper that night the wind sprang up. It increased in violence until, at ten o'clock, there was a howling gale, through which the airship had to fight her way with almost all her available power.

"Some wind!" cried Dick, when he went on duty, and, glancing at the gage noted it to be blowing at seventy miles an hour.

"Luckily it isn't altogether dead against us," said Mr. Vardon. "As it is, though, it's cutting down our speed to about twenty miles an hour, and I don't want to force the engine too much."

"No," agreed Dick. "It isn't worth while, especially as the gale is serving the other craft just as it is us."

CHAPTER XXVIII

ABLAZE IN THE CLOUDS

There was small consolation, however, for those aboard Dick's craft, in the thought that other competing airships were in the same plight as themselves. For, as the night wore on, the wind seemed to increase in power. Only the mechanical strength of the Abaris enabled her to weather the storm.

"We could not possible do it were it not for the gyroscope stabilizer," declared Lieutenant McBride. "We would be on our beams ends all the while. It's a great invention."

"Well, this certainly is a good test of it," agreed Mr. Vardon, with pardonable pride.

Indeed, no more severe strain could have been put upon the apparatus. There would come a great gust of the tornado, and the ship would begin to heel over. But the marvelous power of the gyroscope would force her back again.

On through the night and through the gale went the airship. So severe was the storm that it was not deemed wise for any one to remain in his bunk. So everyone spent the hours of darkness in wakeful watching and waiting.

"We want to be ready to act in any emergency," explained Mr. Vardon. "There's no telling when something may give way under the strain."

"Well, then we ought to go over all the machinery every ten minutes or so, and see if anything is wrong," suggested Dick. "We might see the trouble starting in time to prevent it."

"Good idea!" cried the lieutenant. "We'll make periodical inspections. Everyone on the job, as the boys say."

The task of looking after the machinery was divided up among the young aviators, and, as the craft was swayed this way and that by the gale, eager and anxious eyes watched every revolution of the gear wheels, pistons were minutely inspected in the light of electric torches, and valves adjusted when they showed the least sign of going wrong.

Poor Grit seemed to be afraid, which was something new for him. He would not leave Dick for an instant, but kept at his heels, even when his master went near the sparking motors and dynamos, which the bulldog had good reason to fear. But now he seemed more afraid of something else than the machines that had shocked him.

"I wonder what's the matter?" spoke the young millionaire. "I never saw him act this way before. What is it, old boy?" he asked soothingly.

Grit whined uneasily.

"Sometimes animals have premonitions," said Mr. Vardon. "I remember once, in my early days of flying, I took a dog up with me.

"Everything seemed to be going along fine, but the dog showed signs of uneasiness, though it wasn't on account of the height, for he'd been up before. But it wasn't five minutes later before one of my propeller blades broke off, and I nearly turned turtle before I could make a landing."

"I hope nothing like that occurs now," said Larry. "It might make a good story, but it would be a mighty uncomfortable feeling."

"I don't anticipate anything," said the aviator. "We seem to be doing very well. But we are making scarcely any progress, and we are being blown considerably off our course."

"We'll make it up when the wind stops," Dick said. "I'm determined to win that prize!"

"This is a peculiar storm," Lieutenant McBride observed. "It seems to be nothing but wind. I'm inclined to think there had been an area of low pressure about this region, caused possibly by some other storm, and the air from another region is now rushing in, filling up the partial vacuum."

"In that case we might try to rise above it," suggested Mr. Vardon. "I've often done that. We could go up. It would not be advisable to go down any lower, as we don't want to run the risk of colliding with any mountains, and we are getting pretty well to the Northwest now. Suppose we try to go up?"

This was agreed on as a wise plan, and Dick, who was taking his turn at the wheel, shifted the rudder to send his craft up on a long slant.

But now a new difficulty arose. It seemed that the change in angle made a heavier wind pressure on the big planes, and the speed of the airship was reduced to a bare ten miles an hour. In fact she seemed almost stationary in the air, at times.

"This won't do!" cried Dick. "We've got to turn on more power, even if we do strain the machinery. We've got to have more speed than this!"

"That's right!" cried Mr. Vardon. "I'll turn 'em up, Dick."

And with the increased speed of the big motor that was whirling the propellers came increased danger of a break. Vigilance was redoubled, and they had their reward for their care.

"Here's something wrong!" cried Innis, as he passed a small dynamo that supplied current for the electric lights. "A hot bearing!" and he pointed to where one was smoking.

"Shut down! Quick!" cried Mr. Vardon. "Throw over the storage battery switch. That will run the lights until that shaft cools. It must have run out of oil."

The dynamo was stopped and as the storage battery was not powerful enough to operate all the lights for very long, only part of the incandescents were used, so that the interior of the ship was only dimly lighted.

"Use your portable electric torches to examine the machinery in the dark places," directed the aviator. "We'll use the dynamo again as soon it cools."

This machine, going out of commission, had no effect on the progress of the airship. She was still fighting her way upward, with Dick at the wheel, and Grit crouching uneasily near him. The dog gave voice, occasionally, to pitiful whines.

"What is it, old boy?" asked Dick. "Is something wrong?"

And Grit's manner showed very plainly that there was. But what it was no one could guess.

"How is she coming, Dick?" asked Innis, a little later. "Can I relieve you?"

"No, I'm not tired. It's only a nervous sort of feeling. I feel as if I were trying to push the airship along."

"I know how it is," murmured the cadet.

"But just take it easy. How is she doing?"

"Better, I think. We seem to be gaining a little. If we could only get above the gale we'd be all right. But it's hard forcing her up. I'd just like to know how Uncle Ezra is making out."

As a matter of fact, as Dick learned later, his relative had no easy time of it. He had gotten off in fair weather, and under good circumstances, but engine trouble developed after the first few hours, and, while he and Larson, with the army man, did not have to come down, they could only fly at slow speed.

"I don't know what's the matter with the thing," said Larson. "I'm afraid we'll have to use even a different carburetor."

"What! And spend more money!" cried Uncle Ezra. "I guess not! No, sir! Up to date this machine has cost me nigh on to eleven thousand dollars! I've got it all down."

"But you'll double your money, and have a fine machine to sell to the government," said Larson. "It will be all right. Give me money for a larger carburetor."

"Well, if I have to I have to, I suppose," sighed the miserly old man. "But try and make this one do."

It would not answer, however, and after trying in vain to get more speed out of the craft, Larson was obliged to use one of the two allowed descents, and go down to readjust the motor.

Then when a couple of days had elapsed, though of course this time was not counted any more than in the case of Dick, another start was made. The Larabee, as Uncle Ezra had called his craft, seemed to do better, and at times she showed a spurt of speed that amazed even Larson himself. They passed several who had started ahead of them.

"We're sure to get that prize!" he exulted.

"Well, I cal'alate if we don't there'll be trouble," declared Uncle Ezra, grimly.

Then they had run into the storm, as had Dick's craft, and several other competing ones, and Larson, the army man and Uncle Ezra were in great difficulties. But they forced their machine on.

Of course Dick and his friends knew nothing of this at the time, as several hundred miles then separated the two airships.

Onward and upward went the Abaris. Now and then she seemed to gain on the wind, but it was a hard struggle.

"I think we're going to do it, though," declared Dick, as he went about with the aviator, looking at and testing the various pieces of machinery. "Our speed has gone up a little, and the wind pressure seems less."

"It is; a little," agreed Mr. Vardon. "But what is worrying me is that we'll have a lot of lost time and distance to make up when we get out of this storm. Still, I suppose it can't be helped."

"Indeed not. We're lucky as it is," admitted the young millionaire. "But I'm going to get Innis and make some coffee. I think it will do us all good."

The electric stove was soon aglow, and a little later the aromatic odor of coffee pervaded the cabin of the airship. Some sandwiches were also made.

And thus, while the craft was fighting her way through the gale, those aboard ate a midnight lunch, with as good appetites as though they were on solid ground. For, in spite of the fact that they were in the midst of danger, they were fairly comfortable. True the aircraft was tilted upward, for she was still climbing on a steep slant, but they had gotten used to this. The gyroscope stabilizer prevented any rolling from side to side.

"Maybe Grit is hungry, and that's what's bothering him," said Dick, as he tossed the dog a bit of canned chicken. But though the animal was usually very fond of this delicacy, he now refused it.

"That's queer," mused Dick. "I can't understand that. Something surely must be wrong. I hope he isn't going to be sick."

"Had we better go any higher?" asked Innis, at the wheel, as he noted the hand on the gage. "We're up nearly nine thousand feet now, and—"

"Hold her there!" cried Mr. Vardon. "If we've gone up that far, and we haven't gotten beyond the gale, there isn't much use trying any more. We'll ride it out at that level."

Indeed the Abaris was very high, and some of the party had a little difficulty in breathing. Grit, too, was affected this way, and it added to his uneasiness.

"If we had some means of making the cabin air-tight we could make the air pressure in here just what we wanted it, regardless of the rarefied atmosphere outside," said Dick. "In my next airship I'll have that done."

"Not a bad idea," agreed Mr. Vardon. "It could be arranged."

The night was wearing on, and as the first pale streaks of dawn showed through the celluloid windows of the cabin it was noticed by the wind gage that the force of the gale was slacking.

"We've ridden it out!" exulted Dick. "She's a good old airship after all. Now we can get back on our course. We ought to be crossing the Rockies soon, and then for the last stage of the trip to San Francisco."

"Oh, we've got considerable distance yet to cover," said the aviator. "I fancy we were blown nearly five hundred miles out of our way, and that's going to take us several hours to make good on."

"Still you are doing well," said the army man. "No airship has ever made a trans-continental flight, and there is no speed record to go by. So you may win after all, especially as the storm was so general."

It was rapidly getting light now, and as they looked they saw that they were above the clouds. They were skimming along in a sea of fleecy, white mist.

"First call for breakfast!" cried Dick. His tones had scarcely died away when there came a howl from Grit, who was standing near the compartment of the main motor.

"What is the matter with that dog?" asked Dick, in a puzzled voice. Grit's howl changed to a bark, and at the same moment, Larry Dexter, who was passing, cried out:

"Fire! There's a fire in the motor-room! Where are the extinguishers?"

A black cloud of smoke rushed out, enveloping Grit, who howled dismally.

CHAPTER XXIX

THE RIVAL AIRSHIP

"What did it?"

"Had we better descend?"

"Everybody get busy!"

"Fire extinguishers here!"

These and other confused cries sounded throughout the airship, following Larry's alarm.

"No, don't go down!" shouted Mr. Vardon. "We'll stay up as long as we can. We'll fight the fire in the air—above the clouds!"

"Hold her steady, Innis!" called Dick to his chum, who was at the wheel.

"Steady she is!" was the grim answer.

And while the Abaris was rushing onward those aboard her prepared to fight that most deadly of enemies—fire—and at a terrible disadvantage—nearly ten thousand feet in the air!

Fortunately preparations had been made for this emergency, and a number of portable extinguishers were placed in various places on the walls of the cabin.

These the young aviators now pulled down and rushed with them to the motor compartment, from which the black smoke was pouring in greater volume.

"Look out for a gasolene explosion!" warned the lieutenant. "Is there any of it there?"

"Only a little," answered Mr. Vardon. "The main supply is in the deck tank. But there is a small can in there for priming the cylinders, in case we have to."

"It smells like oil afire," said Larry Dexter.

"That's what it is—probably some oily waste started by spontaneous combustion," said Mr. Vardon.

As he spoke he threw the contents of his extinguisher inside the motor compartment—it was hardly large enough to be called a room. The smoke was so black that no blaze could be seen.

"Open some of the windows!" shouted Paul. "It's choking in here."

"That's right!" agreed Larry, with a cough and a sneeze.

"Stoop down—get near the floor of the cabin," ordered the army lieutenant. "The air is always more pure there."

He, too, emptied the contents of his extinguisher in the compartment, and his example was followed by the others. The smoke seemed to be less now, and much of it went out through the opened windows, which Paul slid back in their groves.

"There's the blaze!" cried Dick, as he saw, through the lessening haze of smoke, some bright, red tongues of fire.

"Douse it!" cried Paul, handing his chum a fresh extinguisher, for Dick had used his.

The young millionaire threw on the chemical powder, for this happened to be that sort of an extinguisher, and almost instantly there followed a sharp explosion.

"Look out!" yelled Dick, ducking instinctively. "I guess this is the end of everything!"

But, to the surprise of all, the motor still kept up its hum, and they could tell, by the "feel" of the craft that she was still progressing. The gale had now almost completely died out, and the Abaris was making good time, and on her proper course, when the fire was discovered.

"The fire is scattered!" Dick yelled, as he rose up and took another look in the motor-room. "I guess it was only that little tank of gasolene that went up." Afterward this was found to be so.

The blazing liquid, however, had scattered all about the motor compartment. Fortunately the walls were of steel, so that the fiery stuff could burn itself out without doing much damage.

"More extinguishers!" yelled Dick, as he saw the spots of fire about the motor. "First thing we know, some of the insulation will be burned off, and we'll have a short circuit!"

The motor-room was almost free of smoke now, and there were only a few scattered spots of fire. Standing in the entrance, Dick threw the contents of several extinguishers inside, as they were passed to him, and he had the satisfaction of seeing the flames gradually choked by the chemical fumes thus released.

"Now I guess we're all right," said Mr. Vardon, when no more fire could be seen. "And the marvel of it is that our motor never stopped!"

"That's the one thing that saved us from making another descent—our last," murmured Dick. "That's sure some motor, all right."

But they were congratulating themselves too soon, it seemed. For, hardly had Dick spoken than the monotonous whine of the powerful machine seemed to weaken in tone. It died out—the high note sunk to a low one, and gradually went out.

"What's up now?" asked Paul, peering over Dick's shoulder. The motor compartment was still too hot to enter with safety, and it was also filled with acrid vapor, from the extinguishers.

"I—I'm afraid it's going to stop," gasped Dick, for he was out of breath from his exertions, and from the excitement of the occasion.

"Stop!" cried Paul. "If she does we'll have to go down!"

And stop the motor did. There was a sort of final groan or gasp, as if of apology, and then the wheels stopped revolving and the big propellers outside the cabin, which had been forcing the craft onward, gradually ceased their motion.

"Quick?" shouted Mr. Vardon. "Throw on the self-starter, Dick! We may catch her before she loses all her momentum!"

"All right!" answered Dick. He made one jump to the switch that put into commission the electrical starter. But he was too late to "catch" the motor. It had died down, and, though the young millionaire made contact after contact with the copper knife-switch, there was no response.

"We're falling!" cried Innis, from the pilot-house, as he noted the height gage, and saw that the hand was constantly receding. "We're falling, Dick!"

"I know it—no help for it," answered our hero, hopelessly.

The Abaris was certainly going down. When the propellers had ceased to urge her forward she began to dip toward the earth, even as a stone falls when the initial impulse from the sling, or the hand of the thrower, is lost.

Foot by foot she dropped, and those aboard her looked helplessly at one another. They had made a brave fight against the fire, but it seemed to have gone for naught. They could not keep up with the motor stalled as it was.

"I guess we'll have to make another landing," said Innis, as he remained at the wheel.

Of course they were entitled to one more, but it would be the last, and a long and hard part of their trans-continental flight was still ahead of them. If they went down this time, and, after making repairs, came up into the air once more, they would not, under the rules, be allowed to land again before reaching San Francisco.

"It's tough luck, but I guess we'll have to do it," said Larry Dexter.

"Maybe not!" Dick cried. "I have an idea."

"What is it? Tell us quick!" begged Innis, for he, as well as all of Dick's friends, wanted to see him win the prize.

"I think the insulation has been burning off some of the wires of the motor," was his answer. "That would make a short circuit and put it out of business. Now if we can only keep afloat long enough to change those wires, we may be able to start the motor again, and keep on our way before we touch ground."

"You've struck it!" cried Mr. Vardon. "Dick, you take charge of the wheel—you and any of your friends you want. I'll look over the motor, and make repairs if I can."

"And they'll have to be made pretty soon," called out Innis from the pilot-house. "We're falling fast."

"Throw her nose up," cried Dick. "That's what we've got to do to save ourselves. We'll volplane down, and maybe we can keep up long enough to have Mr. Vardon put in new wires in place of the burned-out ones. If he can do that, and if we can start the motor—"

"It sounds too good to be true," said Innis. "But get in here, Dick, and see what you can do. You've got to volplane as you never did before."

"And I'm going to do it!" cried the young millionaire.

The motor-room was now free from smoke, and the fire was out. A pile of charred waste in one corner showed where it had started.

"That's the trouble—insulation burned off!" cried Mr. Vardon, as he made a quick inspection. "I think I can fix it, Dick, if you can keep her up long enough. Take long glides. We're up a good height, and that will help solve."

Then began a curious battle against fate, and, not only a struggle against adverse circumstances, but against gravitation. For, now that there was no forward impulse in the airship, she could not overcome the law that Sir Isaac Newton discovered, which law is as immutable as death. Nothing can remain aloft unless it is either lighter than the air itself, or unless it keeps in motion with enough force to overcome the pull of the magnet earth, which draws all things to itself.

I have told you how it is possible for a body heavier than air to remain above the earth, as long as it is in motion. It is this which keeps cannon balls and airships up— motion. Though, of course, airships, with their big spread of surface, need less force to keep them from falling than do projectiles.

And when the motor of an airship stops it is only by volplaning down, or descending in a series of slanting shifts, that accidents are avoided.

This, then, is what Dick did. He would let the airship shoot downward on a long slant, so as to gain as much as possible. Then, by throwing up the head-rudder, he would cause his craft to take an upward turn, thus delaying the inevitable descent.

All the while this was going on Mr. Vardon, aided by Lieutenant McBride, was laboring hard to replace the burned-out wires. He worked frantically, for he knew he had but a few minutes at the best. From the height at which they were when the motor stopped it would take them about ten minutes to reach the earth, holding back as Dick might. And there was work which, in the ordinary course of events, would take twice as long as this.

"I'm only going to make a shift at it," explained the aviator. "If I can only get in temporary wires I can replace them later."

"That's right," agreed the army man.

"How you making it, Dick?" asked Larry, as he came to the door of the pilot-house.

"Well, I've got five hundred feet left. If he can't get the motor going before we go down that far—"

Dick did not finish, but they all knew what he meant.

"Another second and I'll have the last wire in!" cried Mr. Vardon. "Do your best, Dick."

"I'm doing it. But she's dipping down fast."

"Oh, for a dirigible balloon now!" cried the lieutenant. "We could float while making repairs."

But it was useless to wish for that. They must do the best they could under the circumstances.

"There she is! The last wire in!" shouted the aviator. "How much space left, Dick?"

"About two hundred feet!"

"That may do it. Now to see if the self-starter will work!"

Eagerly he made a jump for the switch. He pulled it over. There was a brilliant blue spark, as the gap was closed.

The electrical starter hummed and whined, as if in protest at being obliged to take up its burden again.

Then, with a hum and a roar, the motor that had stalled began to revolve. Slowly at first, but soon gathering speed.

"Throw in the propeller clutch!" yelled Dick. "We're going right toward a hill, and I can't raise her any more."

"In she goes!" yelled Lieutenant McBride, as he pulled on the lever.

There was a grinding of gears as the toothed wheels meshed, and the big wooden propellers began to revolve.

"There she goes!" cried Mr. Vardon.

The Abaris, which had almost touched the earth, began to soar upward under the propelling influence. Dick tilted back the elevating plane as far as he dared.

Had the motive power come in time, or would they land on the hill?

But success was with them. Up went the big airship. Up and up, flying onward. Her fall had been checked.

And only just in time, for they went over the brow of the hill but with a scant twenty feet to spare. So close had they come to making a landing.

"I congratulate you!" cried Lieutenant McBride. "I thought surely you would go down." He had out his pencil and paper to make a note of the time of landing. It would have been the last one allowed, and it would seriously have handicapped Dick. But he had escaped, and still had some reserve to his credit.

"And now I guess we can eat," said the young millionaire, with a sigh of relief.

"A quick bite, only," stipulated Mr. Vardon. "Some of those wires I put in last are a disgrace to an electrician. I want to change them right away. They won't stand the vibration."

"Well, coffee and sandwiches, anyhow," said Dick, and the simple meal was soon in progress.

Steadily the airship again climbed up toward the clouds, from which she had so nearly fallen. And with a sandwich and a cup of coffee beside him, Mr. Vardon worked at the wires, putting in permanent ones in place of the temporary conductors. This could be done without stopping the motor.

"I wonder if it was the fire Grit was anticipating all the while he acted so queer?" asked Innis.

"I don't know—but it was something," Dick said. "I shouldn't wonder but what he did have some premonition of it. Anyhow, you gave the alarm in time, old boy!" and he patted his pet on the back.

Grit waved his tail, and barked. He seemed himself again.

It took some time to make good the damage done by the fire, and it was accomplished as the airship was put back on her course again, and sent forward toward the Pacific coast. They were all congratulating themselves on their narrow escape from possible failure.

It was that same afternoon, when Mr. Vardon had finished his task, that something else happened to cause them much wonderment.

The motor was again in almost perfect condition, and was running well. Most of the party were out on the deck behind the cabin, enjoying the air, for the day had been hot, and they were tired from fighting the tire.

Suddenly Grit, who was in the pilot-house with Dick, ran out into the main cabin, and, looking from one of the windows, which he could do by jumping up in a chair, he began to bark violently.

"Well, what's the matter now?" demanded Dick. "Is it another fire?"

Grit barked so persistently that Dick called to Paul:

"See what ails him; will you? He must have caught sight of something out of the window."

"I should say he had!" yelled Paul, a moment later. "Here's a rival airship after us, Dick!"

CHAPTER XXX

AN ATTACK

Paul's announcement created considerable excitement. Though they had covered a large part of their trip, the young aviators had not yet seen any of their competitors. As a matter of fact, Dick's craft was among the first to get away in the transcontinental race. But he had feared, several times, that he might be overtaken by lighter and speedier machines.

Now, it seemed, his fears were about to be realized. For the big biplane that Grit had first spied, could be none other than one of those engaged in a try for the twenty-thousand-dollar prize. They were now nearing the Rockies, and it was not likely that any lone aviator would be flying in that locality unless he were after the government money.

"Another airship; eh?" cried Dick. "Let me get a look at her! Someone take the wheel, please."

"I'll relieve you," offered Lieutenant McBride, whose official duties allowed him to do this. "Go see if you can make out who she is, Dick."

The approaching craft had come up from the rear, and to one side, so she could not be observed from the pilot-house in front.

Catching up a pair of powerful field-glasses, Dick went to where Paul stood with Grit, looking out of the celluloid window. By this time some of the others had also gathered there.

"It's a big machine all right," murmured Innis.

"And there are three aviators in her," added Paul.

"Can you make out who they are, Dick?" asked Larry Dexter.

"No, they have on protecting helmets and goggles," replied the young millionaire, as he adjusted the binoculars to his vision. "But I'm sure I know that machine!"

"Whose is it?" Innis wanted to know.

"Well, I don't want to be too positive, but I'm pretty certain that's my Uncle Ezra's craft," replied Dick, slowly.

"Great Scott!" cried Paul. "Is it possible? Oh, it's possible all right," Dick made answer, "but I did not think he would really take part in this race. However, he seems to have done so. I can't make him out, but that's just the shape of his airship, I can tell by the mercury stabilizer Larson has put on."

"Well, it looks as if we'd have a race," observed Mr. Vardon.

"He sure is speeding on," mused Dick.

"But he may be away behind his schedule," put in Larry.

"That won't make any difference," the young millionaire said. "He started after we did, and if he gets to San Francisco ahead of us, and with only two landings, he'll win the prize. That stands to reason. He's making better time than we are."

Mr. Vardon took the glasses from Dick, and made a long observation. When he lowered them he remarked:

"I think that is the craft Larson built, all right. And it certainly is a speedy one. He must have met more favorable conditions, of late, than we did, or he never could have caught up to us."

"I guess so," agreed Dick. "Now the point is; What can we do?"

"Speed up—that's the only thing I see to do," came from the aviator. "We still have one landing left us, but we don't need to use it unless we have to. We have fuel and oil enough for the trip to San Francisco. Speed up, I say, and let's see if we can't get away from him."

"We've got a heavier machine, and more weight aboard," spoke Dick.

"Say, can't you drop us off?" cried Paul. "That would lighten you a whole lot. Let Innis and me go!"

"I'll drop off, too, if it will help any," Larry Dexter offered.

"And be killed?" asked Mr. Vardon.

"Not necessarily. You could run the airship over some lake, or river, lower it as close as possible, and we could drop into the water. We can all swim and dive. You could drop us near shore, we could get out and make our way to the nearest town. That would leave you with less load to carry."

174 | P a g e

"I wouldn't think of it!" cried Dick.

"Why not?" asked Innis.

"In the first place I want my airship to do what I built it for—carry this party across the continent. If it can't do that, and in time to at least give me a chance for the government prize, I'm going to have one that can. In the second place, even if your going off would help me to win, I wouldn't let you take the risk.

"No, we'll stick together. I think I can get away from Uncle Ezra, if that's who is in that biplane. We can run up our speed considerable. We haven't touched the extreme limit yet."

"Well, if you won't you won't—that settles it," said Paul. "But if you're going to speed you'd better begin. He is sure coming on."

Indeed the other aircraft was rushing toward them at a rapid rate. It had been some distance in the rear when first sighted, but now the three figures aboard were plainly discernable with the naked eye.

"Speed her up!" called Dick. "We've got to leave him if we can."

Gradually the Abaris forged on more rapidly. But it seemed as if those in the other craft were waiting for something like this. For they, too, put on more power, and were soon overhauling the larger airship.

"They've got an awful lot of force in a light craft," observed Lieutenant McBride. "She's over engined, and isn't safe. Even if your uncle gets in ahead of you, Dick, I will still maintain that you have the better outfit, and the most practical. I don't see how they can live aboard that frail craft."

It certainly did not look very comfortable, and afterward Uncle Ezra confessed that he endured many torments during the trip.

The race was on in earnest. They were over the Rockies now, and at the present rate of speed it would be only a comparatively short time before they would be at the Pacific coast.

"If I only knew how many landings he had made I wouldn't be so worried," said Dick. "If he's had more than two he's out of it, anyhow, and I wouldn't strain my engine."

"We'd better keep on," advised Mr. Vardon, and they all agreed to this.

175 | P a g e

Toward the close of the afternoon the Larabee, which they were all sure was the name of the craft in the rear, came on with a rush. Her speed seemed increased by half, and she would, it was now seen, quickly pass the Abaris.

"Well, they're going ahead of us," sighed Dick. "Uncle Ezra did better than I thought he would."

Neither he nor any of the others were prepared for what happened. For suddenly the other airship swooped toward Dick's craft, in what was clearly a savage attack. Straight at the Abaris, using all her speed, came Uncle Ezra's airship.

CHAPTER XXXI

THE WRECK

"What do they mean?"

"What's their game, anyhow?"

"They'll ram us if they don't look out!"

"Maybe they've lost control of her!"

"Dick, if that's your uncle, tell him to watch where he's going!"

Thus cried those aboard the aircraft of the young millionaire as they watched the oncoming of the rival craft. She was certainly coming straight at them. It was intentional, too, for Mr. Vardon, who was at the wheel of the Abaris, quickly changed her course when he saw what was about to happen, and the other pilot could have had plenty of room to pass in the air.

Instead he altered his direction so as to coincide with that of Dick's craft.

"They must be crazy!"

"If they'll hit us we'll go to smash, even if she is a lighter machine than ours!"

Thus cried Paul and Innis as they stood beside Dick.

"It's my Uncle Ezra, all right," murmured the wealthy youth. "I can recognize him now, in spite of his helmet and goggles. But what in the world is he up to, anyhow? He can't really mean to ram us, but it does look so."

The two airships were now but a short distance apart, and in spite of what Mr. Vardon could do, a collision seemed inevitable. The fact of the matter was that the Larabee, being smaller and lighter, answered more readily to her rudders than did the Abaris.

"We've got to have more speed, Dick!" called the aviator. "I'm going to turn about and go down. It's the only way to get out of their way. They're either crazy, or bent on their own destruction, as well as ours. Give me more speed, Dick! All you can!"

"All right!" answered the young millionaire. "We'll do our best to get out of your way, Uncle Ezra!"

As Dick hastened to the motor-room, Grit trotted after him, growling in his deep voice at the mention of the name of the man he so disliked.

Dick realized the emergency, and turned the gasolene throttle wide open. With a throb and a roar, the motor took up the increase, and whirled the big propellers with mighty force.

Then, in a last endeavor to prevent the collision, Mr. Vardon sent the craft down at a sharp slant, intending to dive under the other.

But this move was anticipated by Larson, who was steering the Larabee.

He, too, sent his craft down, but just when a collision seemed about to take place, it was prevented by Mr. Vardon, who was a more skillful pilot.

The propellers of the Abaris worked independently, on a sort of differential gear, like the rear wheels of an automobile. This enabled her to turn very short and quickly, by revolving one propeller in one direction, and one in the opposite, as is done with the twin screws of a steamer.

And this move alone prevented what might have been a tragedy. But it was also the cause of a disaster to Dick's aircraft.

With a rush and a roar the Larabee passed over the Abaris as she was so suddenly turned, and then something snapped in the machinery of the big airship. She lost speed, and began to go down slightly.

"Did they hit us?" cried Dick, in alarm.

"No, but we've broken the sprocket chain on the port propeller," answered Mr. Vardon.

"We'll have to be content with half speed until we can make repairs. Come now, everybody to work. Those crazy folks may come back at us—that is begging your pardon for calling your uncle crazy, Dick."

"You can't offend me that way. He MUST be crazy to act the way he did. I can't understand it. Of course Larson was steering, but my uncle must have given him orders to do as he did, and try to wreck us."

"I shall report whoever the army man was that did not make an attempt to stop their attack on us," declared Lieutenant McBride, bitterly. "I don't know who was assigned to the Larabee, but he certainly ought to be court-martialed."

"Perhaps no army representative was aboard at all," suggested Paul.

"There were three persons on the airship," said Larry. "I saw them."

"And the race would not be counted unless an army representative was aboard," declared Lieutenant McBride. "So they would not proceed without one. No, he must have been there, and have entered into their plot to try and wreck us. I can't understand it!"

"They've evidently given it up, whatever their game was," called Innis. "See, there they go!"

He pointed to the other airship, which was now some distance away, going on at good speed, straight for San Francisco. Both craft were now high in the air, in spite of the drop made by the Abaris, and they were about over some of the mountains of Colorado now; just where they had not determined. They were about eight hundred miles from San Francisco, as nearly as they could calculate.

"They're trying to get in first," said Dick. "Maybe, after all, they just wanted to frighten us, and delay us."

"Well, if that was their game they've succeeded in delaying us," said Mr. Vardon, grimly. "We're reduced to half speed until we get that propeller in commission again. There's work for all of us. Reduce sped, Dick, or we may tear the one good blade off the axle."

With only half the resistance against it, the motor was now racing hard. Dick slowed it down, and then the work of repairing the broken sprocket chain and gear was undertaken.

It was not necessary to stop the airship to do this. In fact to stop meant to descend, and they wanted to put that off as long as possible. They still had the one permitted landing to their credit.

The propellers, as I have said, could be reached from the open deck, and thither Mr. Vardon, Dick, and Lieutenant McBride took themselves, while Paul, Innis and Larry would look after the progress of the craft from the pilot-house and motor-room.

Slowly Dick's airship went along, just enough speed being maintained to prevent her settling. She barely held her own, while, far ahead of her, and fast disappearing in the distance, could be seen the other craft—that carrying Uncle Ezra.

"I guess it's all up with us," murmured Paul, as he went to the wheel.

"No, it isn't!" cried Dick. "I'm not going to give up yet! We can still make time when we get the repairs made, and I'll run the motor until her bearings melt before I give up!"

"That's the way to talk!" cried the army man. "And we're all with you. There's a good chance yet, for those fellows must be desperate, or they'd never have tried what they did. My opinion is that they hope to reach San Francisco in a last dash, and they were afraid we'd come in ahead of them. But I can't understand how that army man aboard would permit such a thing. It is past belief!"

It was no easy task to make the repairs with the airship in motion. Spare parts, including a sprocket chain, were carried aboard, but the work had to be done close to the other revolving propeller, and, as slowly as it was whirling about, it went fast enough to cause instant death to whoever was hit by it. So extreme caution had to be used.

To add to the troubles it began to rain violently, and a thunderstorm developed, which made matters worse. Out in the pelting storm, with electrically-charged clouds all about them, and vivid streaks of lightning hissing near them, the aviators worked.

They were drenched to the skin. Their hands were bruised and cut by slipping wrenches and hammers. Their faces were covered with black grease, dirt and oil. But still they labored on. The storm grew worse, and it was all the Abaris could do to stagger ahead, handicapped as she was by half power.

But there were valiant hearts aboard her, and everyone was imbued with indomitable courage.

"We're going to do it!" Dick cried, fiercely, and the others echoed his words.

Finally, after many hours of work, the last rivet was driven home, and Mr. Vardon cried:

"There we are! Now then, full speed ahead!"

The repaired propeller was thrown into gear. It meshed perfectly, and once more the Abaris shot ahead under her full power.

"Speed her up!" cried Dick, and the motor was put to the limit. But much precious time had been lost. Could they win under such adverse circumstances? It was a question each one asked himself.

Darkness came on, and the tired and weary aviators ate and slept. The night passed, a clear, calm night, for the storm had blown itself out. High over the mountains soared the airship through the hours of darkness. She was fighting to recover what she had lost.

And when morning came they calculated they were but a few hundred miles from San Francisco.

Paul, who had gone to the pilot-house to relieve Innis, gave a startled cry.

"Look! Look!" he shouted. "There's the other airship!"

And as the others looked they saw, ahead of them, emerging from the midst of a cloud, Uncle Ezra's speedy craft. And, as they looked, they saw something else— something that filled them with horror.

For, as they gazed at the craft which had so nearly, either by accident or design, wrecked them, they saw one of the big side planes crumple up, as does a bird's broken wing. Either the supports had given way, or a sudden gust of air strained it too much.

"They're falling!" cried Dick, hoarsely.

The other airship was. The broken plane gave no support on that side, and as the motor still raced on, whirling the big propellers, the Larabee, unevenly balanced, in spite of the mercury stabilizers, tilted to one side.

Then, a hopeless wreck, she turned over and plunged downward toward the earth. Her race was over.

CHAPTER XXXII

SAVING UNCLE EZRA

For a moment those aboard Dick's airship uttered not a sound. Then, as they saw the rival craft sifting slowly downward, gliding from side to side like a sheet of paper, they looked at one another with horror in their eyes. It seemed such a terrible end.

Dick was the first to speak.

"We'll have to go down and help them," he said simply. "Some of them may be—alive!"

It meant stopping the race, it meant making the last of the two landings allowed them. And it was a landing in a wild and desolate place, seemingly, for there was no sign of city or town below them. And just now, after her repairs, when everything was running smoothly, it behooved Dick and his associates to take advantage of every mile and minute they could gain. Otherwise some other craft might get in ahead of them.

Yet Dick had said they must go down. There was no other course left them, in the name of humanity. As the young millionaire had observed, some of those in the wrecked airship might be alive. They might survive the fall, great as it was.

"Send her down, Mr. Vardon," said Dick quietly. "We may be able to save some of them."

If he thought that possibly he was losing his last chance to win the trans-continental race, he said nothing about it.

The motor was shut off, and there was silence aboard the Abaris. No one felt like talking. As they volplaned downward they saw the wreck of the Larabee strike the outer branches of a big tree, and then turn over again before crashing to the ground.

"She may catch fire from the gasolene," said Dick, in a tense voice. "We ought to hurry all we can."

"I could go down faster," said Mr. Vardon, "by starting up the motor. But I don't like to until I see what sort of landing ground we'll have."

"No, it's wiser to go a bit slowly," agreed Lieutenant McBride. "We must save ourselves in order to save them—if possible. It's a terrible accident!"

As they came nearer earth they saw a comparatively smooth and level spot amid a clearing of trees. It was not far from where the wreck lay, a crumpled-up mass. Down floated the Abaris gently, and hardly had she ceased rolling along on her wheels that Dick and the others rushed out to lend their aid to Uncle Ezra and the others.

Dick's uncle lay at some little distance from the broken craft.

"He's alive," said his nephew, feeling of the old man's heart. "He's still breathing."

Lieutenant Wilson, as the name of the army officer on the Larabee was learned later to be, seemed quite badly injured. He was tangled up in the wreckage, and it took some work to extricate him. Larson was the most severely hurt. He was tenderly placed to one side. Fortunately the wreck had not caught fire.

"Let's see if we can revive them," suggested Lieutenant McBride, nodding toward Uncle Ezra and his fellow soldiers. "Then we will consider what is best to do."

Simple restoratives were carried aboard Dick's airship, and these were given to Uncle Ezra, who revived first. He opened his eyes and sat up.

"Where—where am I?" he stammered. "Did I win the race?"

"No, Uncle Ezra, I'm sorry to say you didn't," answered Dick, gently. "There was an accident, and your airship is smashed."

The old man slowly looked over to the crumpled mass of planes and machinery, and then, slowly and painfully, for he was much bruised, he pulled a note-book from his pocket. Leafing over the pages he announced:

"Busted to smithereens, and she cost me exactly eleven thousand five hundred and thirty-three dollars and nineteen cents! Oh, what a lot of money!" And the expression on his face was so painful that Dick felt inclined to laugh, solemn as the occasion was. But he restrained himself.

"Where's that fellow Larson?" asked Uncle Ezra.

"Badly hurt," said Dick, quietly.

"Oh, well, then I won't say anything," murmured the old man. "Oh, what a trip it was!"

"Are you much hurt?" asked Dick.

It did not appear that his uncle was. The fall had been a lucky one for him. His helmet had protected his head, and he had on two suits of clothes, well padded. The others were dressed likewise, but it had not saved Larson.

Lieutenant Wilson's most serious injury was a broken leg, but he was also otherwise hurt. He soon recovered consciousness, and said:

"Please don't misjudge me. I could not stop Larson from trying to ram you. He was insane, I guess. We have had a terrible time with him. He was mad to try to win this race. We remonstrated with him when he sailed toward you, but he said he was only trying to show you what a superior machine he had, and how much better his mercury stabilizers worked than your gyroscope. But I really fear he meant you some injury."

"I think so, too," said Lieutenant McBride, "and I am glad to learn no one else was in the plot."

"And his own foolish actions were the cause of this wreck," went on Lieutenant Wilson. "He said he was sure of winning after he had left you behind, and he wanted to try some experiments in quick turns. He made one too quick, and broke off one of the planes."

"Well, we must consider what is to be done," said Mr. Vardon. "We must get you all to a hospital and a doctor, at once."

"Don't mind about me," replied Lieutenant Wilson, gamely. "If you can send me help, do so, but don't delay here. Go on and win the race. You have the best chance, I believe."

"We don't go on until we see you cared for," spoke Dick. "We would take you all with us, only it might endanger you."

"Well, I wish you'd take me!" exclaimed Uncle Ezra, limping about. "I want to get back home. Nephew Richard, I'm sorry I tried to beat you in this race."

"That's all right, Uncle Ezra," answered the young millionaire. "You had as good a right to try for the prize as I did."

"But I want to say I didn't have no hand in trying to butt into you," went on Mr. Larabee. "It was all that—that unfortunate man's idea," he added more softly, as he gazed at Larson who was still unconscious. "Dick, will you forgive me, and shake hands?"

"Surely, Uncle Ezra," and as their hands met, Grit, who had been eyeing Mr. Larabee narrowly, uttered a joyful bark, and actually wagged his tail at Uncle Ezra.

"Grit, you shake hands, too," ordered Dick, and though Uncle Ezra was a little diffident at first, he grasped the extended paw of the bulldog. They were friends for the first time.

"We could take Uncle Ezra in the airship," said Paul, after a pause, "and if we could only send out a call for help for Lieutenant Wilson and Larson, they would be looked after."

"There's an army post not far from here," spoke Wilson. "If you could make a trip there—"

"We'd have to land again, to summon aid, and this is the last stop we are allowed in the race," said Mr. Vardon. "I don't see how—"

"Your wireless!" interrupted Lieutenant McBride. "We can send out a call to the army post by that—if they have a wireless station."

"They have," answered Lieutenant Wilson, as his fellow officer looked at him. "If you will summon aid from there, we will be well taken care of."

"Good!" cried Dick. "That problem is solved."

The wireless apparatus was brought out, the small balloon inflated, and it carried aloft the aerials. Then, while the call for aid was being sent out, Lieutenants Wilson and Larson were made as comfortable as possible, and some of Uncle Ezra's scratches and bruises were looked after.

"No more airships for me," he said bitterly, though with a chastened spirit. "I'm going to stick to farming, and my woolen mill. Just think of it—over eleven thousand dollars in that pile of—junk!" and he shook his head sadly at the wreck of his airship.

"We'll take you on to San Francisco with us, if you like," said Dick. "You can see us win the race—if we can," he added.

"You still have an excellent chance," said Lieutenant McBride. "My advice to you would be to remain here a few days to rest up and make sure all your machinery is in good order. The time will not count against you. By that time the injured ones will be cared for. Then you can go on again and complete the course. You have enough oil and gasolene, have you not?"

"We could ask that some be brought from the army post, if we have not," Dick answered. "I think we will adopt that plan."

"And I—I hope you win," said Uncle Ezra. "I'd like to see that twenty thousand dollars come into the family, anyhow," he added, with a mountainous sigh.

CHAPTER XXXIII

WITH UNCLE EZRA'S HELP

"We're off!"

"On the last lap!"

"No more landings!"

Thus cried Innis, Paul and Larry as they stood in the cabin of the airship. Once more they were on the flight.

"This train makes no stops this side of San Francisco!" cried Dick Hamilton, after the manner of the conductor of a Limited. "That is, I hope we don't," he added with a grim smile. "If we do it will cost me twenty thousand dollars."

"Quite an expensive stop," observed Lieutenant McBride.

"Don't think of it!" said Uncle Ezra. "Nephew Richard, after my failure, you've just GOT to win that prize."

"I'll try," Dick answered.

It was several days after the events narrated in the last chapter. The wireless, sending out its crackling call, had brought speedy help from the army post, and the two lieutenants were taken to the hospital by their fellow soldiers.

Larson recovered consciousness before Dick and his friends left, but was delirious, and practically insane. They had to bind him with ropes to prevent him doing himself and others an injury. His mind had been affected for some time, it was believed.

Some time later, I am glad to say, he recovered, in a sanitorium, though he was always lame from the accident. He was a much different man, however, and begged Dick's forgiveness for trying to collide with him. Lieutenant Wilson made a quick recovery, and, in spite of the mishap, still kept up his interest in aviation, winning much fame for himself.

The army officers, who came to attend the injured ones, brought Dick some supplies and gasolene.

Uncle Ezra begged that some part of his wrecked airship be saved, but it was impossible. There was little left that was worth anything, and Dick, by taking his uncle as an extra passenger, added enough weight as it was, so that no parts of the Larabee could be taken along.

"I might have saved a little," said Uncle Ezra, with a sigh. "I've lost a pile of money!" But he realized that it was out of the question.

The Abaris had been gone over minutely, and put in excellent shape for her final dash. She was taken to the edge of a sloping table-land and there once more launched into space. Before that, however, Lieutenant Wilson had been taken back to the army post, and Larson sent to the hospital. Lieutenant Wilson wished Dick and his friends all sorts of good luck.

Then, with Uncle Ezra aboard, the start was made. There was some crowding, because of the extra passenger, and his valise, which he insisted on bringing with him, but this could be borne.

"We ought to make San Francisco in three hours now," said Dick, when they were up in the air once more.

Uncle Ezra was frankly delighted with his nephew's craft. He did not even say it was wasteful, when Dick told him how much she cost.

"I know airships are terrible expensive—terrible!" said Mr. Larabee, as he looked at the note-book in which he had jotted down every item of money paid for his own.

That Larson had wasted money, and used much of what was given him for his own purposes was very evident. But it was too late to think of that now.

Uncle Ezra told of their experiences in crossing the continent. They had really had excellent luck, and in the hands of a better aviator, or one more dependable, the Larabee might have won the race. She was really a good biplane, but could only carry three, and then with no comfort at all, as compared to Dick's. But the mercury stabilizers worked fairly well, though not as good as the gyroscope.

"Yes, I was sorry, more than once, that I ever left Dankville," Uncle Ezra said, "but Larson wouldn't let me stop. He kept right on. I'm sure he was crazy."

On and on rushed the Abaris. She was racing against time now, and every minute and mile counted. While down on the ground, helping save Uncle Ezra, Dick had, by wireless, communicated with the army authorities in San Francisco, telling them he was coming on the last stage, and asking that a landing-place be designated. This was done, Presido Park Reservation, on the outskirts of the city being named as the spot where the craft could officially come down.

"We'll soon be there," remarked Dick, who was at the wheel. It was afternoon, and by computation they were not more than ninety miles from their goal.

"See anything of any other craft?" asked Paul of his chum.

"Take a look, Innis," suggested the young millionaire. "We might get a race at the last minute."

Innis swept the horizon with the glasses.

"There's something coming behind us," he said. "I can't tell whether it's a big bird, or an airship."

A little later, however, the speck in the blue sky was made out to be a big biplane, rushing onward.

"They're probably trying for the prize," said Dick. "Of course we don't know anything about their time and stops, but, just the same, I'm going to beat her in, if I can. We'll run the motor under forced speed, Mr. Vardon, and feed her heated gasolene."

"That's the idea!" cried the aviator. "That ought to help some."

The motor was so adjusted as to take heated gasolene, the liquid vaporizing and exploding better than when cold. The Abaris rushed on at increased speed.

But so, also, came on behind her the other airship. As Dick had said, that craft might have no chance, having used up more than her limit of stops, or having consumed more elapsed time than had he. But, for all that, he was taking no chances.

The other craft was a swift one. That was easily seen as it slowly crept up on Dick. The speed of each was terrific. The gages showed ninety-five miles an hour for the Abaris. At that rate the city of Oakland, just across the bay from San Francisco, was soon sighted.

And then something happened that nearly put Dick out of the race. His motor suddenly stopped, and all efforts to start it proved futile.

"We've got to go down!" cried our hero, "and within sight of the goal, too! This is fierce!"

"What's the trouble?" asked Larry.

"Not a drop of gasolene left!" said Mr. Vardon, with a tragic gesture, as he made an examination. "There's a leak in the tank. We haven't a drop left. The vibration must have opened a seam and we've been spilling our fuel as we went along."

"There goes the other airship!" cried Innis, as the big biplane flashed by them. They had now crossed Oakland and the bay.

"And the Presido Park is in sight!" yelled Paul, pointing to a big field, now black with people, for the coming of Dick had been flashed all over San Francisco and Oakland.

"We can never make it," the young millionaire murmured. "We'll have to volplane down, but we can't reach the park. Oh, for a gallon of gasolene! One gallon would do!"

"What's that!" cried Uncle Ezra, coming from his bunk room. "What do you want of gasolene?"

"To complete the trip," cried Dick. "Ours is all gone! A gallon would do."

"Then, by hickory, you shall have it!" suddenly cried Mr. Larabee.

"Where can you get it?" demanded Dick. "There isn't a drop aboard!

"Oh, yes there is!" his uncle answered. "Here it is," and he brought from his room a square, gallon can.

"Great Scott!" cried Dick, as he took it and hurried with it toward the empty tank. "Where in the world did you get it?"

"I brought it along in my valise to clean the grease spots off my clothes," answered Uncle Ezra, simply. "I got all oil from my airship. But I wasn't going to buy a new suit when I could clean my old one."

"Whoop!" cried Dick, with boyish enthusiasm. "This may save the race for us."

The Abaris had already begun to settle down, but a moment later, as the motor received the supply of gasolene so Providentially provided, she shot forward again, her momentum scarcely checked.

On and on she rushed. It was nip and tuck now between her and the rival airship. The big crowd in the aviation field yelled and shouted at the sight of the thrilling race.

The other airship seemed to falter and hesitate. The pilot cut off his motor, but too soon. Dick rushed his craft on, passed the other, and then, seeing that he had the advantage, he turned off his power, and volplaned to the landing spot just about fifteen seconds in advance of his rival. He had beaten in the race at the last minute. But it still remained to be seen whether he had triumphed over other, and possibly previous, arrivals.

Out of the Abaris rushed the young millionaire and his friends before she had ceased rolling over the ground. The other biplane was just behind them.

An army officer ran out of the crowd of spectators.

"Who is the pilot of this craft?" he asked.

"I am," answered Dick.

"And where is your official army timekeeper?"

"Here," answered Lieutenant McBride, saluting. "Are we the first to cross the continent?"

How anxiously Dick waited for the answer. "No, not the first," replied the San Francisco officer. "One biplane arrived yesterday. What is your time?"

Lieutenant McBride made a hasty calculation.

"Sixty-two hours, forty minutes and fourteen seconds from, New York, taking out the time of two landings," was the reply.

"Then you win!" cried Captain Weston, as he introduced himself. "That is, unless this other craft can better your time. For the first arrival was seventy-two hours altogether."

And Dick had won, for the biplane with which he had just had the exciting race, had consumed more than eighty hours, exclusive of stops, from coast to coast.

"Hurray, Dick! You win!" cried Innis, clapping his chum on the back.

"The best trans-continental flight ever made!" declared Captain Weston, as he congratulated the young millionaire.

"I'd like to have gotten here first," murmured Dick.

"Well, you'd have been here first, only for the delay my airship caused you," said Uncle Ezra. "I'm sorry."

"But you get the prize," spoke Lieutenant McBride.

"Yes," assented Captain Weston, of Fort Mason. "It was the time that counted, not the order of arrival. Which reminds me that you may yet be beaten, Mr. Hamilton, for there are other airships on the way."

But Dick was not beaten. His nearest competitor made a poorer record by several hours, so Dick's performance stood.

And that, really, is all there is to tell of this story, except to add that by the confession of Larson, later it was learned that he had tampered with Mr. Vardon's gyroscope, as had been suspected. The twenty thousand dollars was duly paid, and Dick gave the United States government an option to purchase his patents of the Abaris. For them he would receive a substantial sum, and a large part of this would go to Mr. Vardon for his gyroscope.

"So you'll be all right from now on," his cousin Innis remarked.

"Yes, thanks to your friend Dick Hamilton. My good luck all dates from meeting him."

"Yes, he is a lucky chap," agreed Paul.

"I think Uncle Ezra had all the luck this trip," put in Dick, as he heard the last words. "That gasolene he brought along to clean the grease off his clothes saved our bacon, all right. It sure did!"

And I believe Dick was right.

Mr. Hamilton, to whom Dick wired a brief message of the successful ending of the trip, telegraphed back:

"Congratulations. You made good after all. I haven't any doubts now."

"That's another time I put one over on dad!" laughed Dick.

"Where are you going, Larry?" asked the young millionaire, as he saw his young newspaper friend hurrying across the aviation field.

"I'm going to wire the story to the Leader," was the answer. "I want 'em to know we crossed the continent and won the prize. It'll be a great beat!"

Of how Dick was feted and greeted by an aviation club in San Francisco, of how he was made much of by the army officers, and how he had to give many exhibition flights, I will say nothing here, as this book is already lengthy enough. Sufficient to remark that the young millionaire had a great time at the City of the Golden Gate, and Uncle Ezra and his friends enjoyed it with him. Grit, also, came in for a share of attention.

Dick Hamilton left his airship with the San Francisco army officers, as he had agreed to do, for they wanted to study its construction. In due season, the party started back East.

"I rather calculated you'd go back in the airship," said Uncle Ezra. "Railroad fare is terrible expensive, and I've lost so much money already—"

"I'll buy your ticket," said Dick generously, "especially as you helped me win the race," and Mr. Larabee, with a look of relief on his face, put back his pocketbook.

"And now for Hamilton Corners!" exclaimed Dick, as they got in the train. "I've had enough of airships for a while, though it was great sport." And here we will take leave of Dick Hamilton and his friends.

End of the book.